I0012475

M 1 CHIP MACBOOK PRO USER GUIDE

THE ULTIMATE BEGINNER'S MANUAL TO USING THE LATEST M 1 CHIP MACBOOK PRO WITH TIPS AND TRICKS

BY

FELIX O. COLLINS

Copyright © 2021 FELIX O. COLLINS

LEGAL NOTICE:

Contents

INTRODUCTION

The 13-inch MacBook Pro (M1 2020) could be one of Apple's best versions so far. Great internal fixes by leaving Apple's Intel use for the well-known 5-nanometer M1 chip (the same chip that powers the MacBook Air (M1, 2020) and Mac mini (M1, 2020)), the smaller MacBook Pro Function is much more powerful than that. That used to be the case.

This sleek M1 chip allows the new 13-inch MacBook Pro to offer better performance than its previous Intel - to be precise, three times faster than comparable Windows laptops and 2.8 times faster than before. Best of all, it makes it use more power, making the battery life longer than its predecessor Intel. At least, that's what Apple promised.

We've found its effectiveness in native systems and in using older versions of Intel-based MacBooks, which have left deep thinking, and the 13-inch Apple MacBook Pro (2020 M1) performance has shocked us. If you're worried that Apple's MacBook will lose functionality due to leaving Intel, this is not the case.

The 256GB SSD / 8GB RAM model starts at US $ 1,299 / £ 1,299 / AU $ 1,999, similar to the previous model.The MacBook Pro 13-inch (M1, 2020) is a much cheaper computer, with the Dell XPS 13 (late 2020)) One of the biggest competitors, the price has been reduced by $ 100 / kg.

The 13-inch MacBook Pro (M1, 2020) is a new exciting redesign of the MacBook Pro series. The bring up to date of the 16-inch model last year is a change of look, with a larger screen, better speakers, and a new keyboard. For the MacBook Pro 13-inch (M1, 2020), the change is all about the interior.

The M1 chip can significantly improve performance and battery life while being able to take advantage of existing Mac apps, brand new apps, and iOS apps with power, and this combined .

with the most competitive, 13-inch production laptop price.

If you at present like the look and feel of the 13-inch MacBook Pro, then you will enjoy this new product. However, we hope that Apple has a lot of facts about design.

MacBook Pro at a glance

Visit MacBook Pro

Note: This guide applies to 13-inch and 16-inch MacBook Pro models currently being shipped. If you are unsure which model you have, or want to get information and documentation for other models, please refer to the Apple Support article "Identify MacBook Pro Model". Not all MacBook Pro models offer all the features.

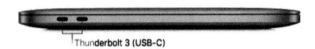

Thunderbolt 3 (USB-C)

- Thunderbolt 3 (USB-C) port: Charge the computer, transfer data at Thunderbolt speed (up to 40 Gbps), connect to a monitor or projectors, etc. On a 13-inch MacBook Pro with an Apple M1 chip, these ports also support USB 4 bandwidth.

3.5 mm headphone jack

- 3.5 mm jack: Connect stereo headphones or external speakers to listen to your favorite music or movies. On the 16-inch MacBook Pro model, the woofer speaker delivers rich bass almost without vibration.
- Microphone: Record live music anytime, anywhere, make conference calls, and mix audio. The three-dimensional microphone configuration of the 13-inch MacBook Pro with Apple M1 chip and 16-inch MacBook Pro offers high-quality studio recording with high signal-to-noise and beamforming direction.

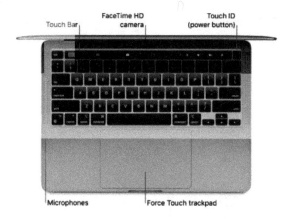

• Touch Bar: The touch bar above the keyboard is highly dynamic in the application you are using. The Touch Bar is a keyboard extension, which can show precise short-cuts and app controls when and where you need them. You can use standard gestures, such as swiping and tap-ping on the touch bar. See MacBook Pro-Magic control panel using Touch Bar and Touch ID.

• FaceTime HD Camera: Make FaceTime video calls or take photos and videos. When the indicator light is on, it means the camera is on. Check out FaceTime.

• Touch ID (power button): Press to use power on MacBook Pro (either simply lift the cover or press any key). When you start or restart for the first time, you need to enter a password to log in. To learn more about how to use Touch ID, see the MacBook Pro-Magic control panel with Touch Bar and Touch ID.

• Force touch trackpad: Use gestures to control MacBook Pro. Every touchpad is like a button, so you can easily click anywhere. For more information on touch, see the MacBook Pro trackpad.

Use Touch Bar in MacBook Pro

Touch Bar is included in many MacOS programs and can provide you with very simple shortcuts based on your current applications and functions. At work, use regular gestures (such as tap and swipe) on the touch bar.

Button to the right of the touch bar to control the controls. You can use them to expand or collapse control bars, change brightness and volume, or use Siri. Some buttons on the touch bar depend on the application you are using.

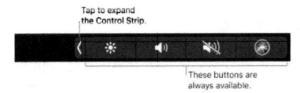

Expand or drop the control bar. The most widely used system controls (such as volume and light) are located in the control bar to the right of the touch bar. Tap the magnification button to extend the thread, then tap the button or slide setting you want to change. After completing the operation, press the X button, or keep the control bar open to keep the buttons available.

Custom control bar. Click "Keyboard" in "System Preferences", then click "Create Control Bar" Drag controls at the bottom of the screen and enter the touch bar to add them. In "Keyboard Preferences", you can also select options for what the control bar displays, such as keys or desktop space.

Show performance keys. Press and hold the function key (Fn) to display the function keys F1 to F12 in the touch bar, then click the task button to use it.

Use the Esc button. The Esc key usually appears on the left side of the touch bar, and the Esc key appears in the same location on the traditional keyboard. Even if some of the tools in the touch bar change, Esc will appear on the left.

Click instead for type. In applications where you write text, such as Notes, Messages, TextEdit, and Email, Touch Bar can display typing suggestions, helping you save time by displaying words and emoji that you can touch instead of typing. If the suggestions for installation are not yet displayed, click the "Predictive Text" button on the touch bar to see suggestions.

Note: Typing suggestions may not be available in all languages or regions.

Express yourself with emojis. In some applications, you can select an emoji instead of text to express your opinion in a fun way. Tap the emoji button to display the emoji. Swipe to scroll through the category-organized options, such as "Frequently Used", "Smiles With People", "Travel & Places", etc. Tap to hand-picked the emoji you want.

Check it out and try it out. Tap once to see tasks that can be completed quickly and efficiently. Touching the touch bar is often easier than clicking or selecting items on the screen to complete tasks or apply settings. For example, turn on the calculator and use the number keys and the touch bar to perform quick calculations without moving the cursor, click and type on the screen.

Keep using the touch bar to find the best way to get the results you want. Move seamlessly between the touch bar, keyboard, and touchpad to complete the task. For details about its bar functionality, see the apps that come with the Mac and the category of each application.

MacBook Pro-Magic Control panel with Touch Bar and Touch ID

The Touch Bar at the top of the Magic keyboard displays a set of tools that will change according to your actions. Touch ID (power switch) is located on the right adjacent to the touch bar. After setting up Touch ID, you can use fingerprints to unlock your MacBook Pro, quickly lock the screen, or shop in the App Store, Apple TV apps, Bookstore, and websites that use Apple Pay.

You can set Touch ID during the setup process, or you can set it later in the Touch of Preferences System System window. To set keyboard and touch preferences, open "System Preferences", click "Keyboard", and then click the up button to see the available options.

Use Touch ID (power button). Press to turn on the power of the MacBook Pro (either just lift the top cover or press any key). When you start or restart your computer for the first time, you need to enter a password to log in. After the initial setup and login, whenever a password is required, you can gently place your finger on the Touch ID verification sensor.

Press the Touch ID sensor to quickly lock the MacBook Pro screen.

You can also use Touch ID to make secure online purchases

through Apple Pay. For more information on Touch ID, see Setting MacBook Pro. For more information on Apple Pay, see the use of Apple Pay on Mac.

Note: To turn off MacBook Pro, select the "Apple" menu> "Shut Down". To sleep MacBook Pro, select menu "Apple"> "Sleep".

All program functions are available in the touch bar.

- Light Button: Press the brightness button or the light button to reduce or increase the brightness of the screen.
- Task control button: Press the control button to view content running on the MacBook Pro, including all openings and open windows.
- Launch button: Press the unlock button to open the launchpad and take a quick look at all the apps on the MacBook Pro. Click the app to open it.
- Keyboard light switch: Press the light key down or increase the light key to reduce or increase keyboard brightness.
- Media button: press the fast return button to go back, press the play/pause button to play or pause, or press the forward button to speed up a song, movie, or slideshow.
- Silence button: Press the mute button to mute the built-in speaker or 3.5 mm headphone jack.
- Volume buttons: Press the volume down or volume down button to decrease or increase the volume of the built-in speaker or 3.5 mm headphone jack.
- Function (Fn) key: Each operating system on the first line can also perform other functions—for example, the F11 key can hide all open windows and display the desktop. When you press the activation key, press and hold the Fn key to start the operation corresponding to the button.
- Function (Fn) / Globe basic: On a 13-inch MacBook Pro with an Apple M1 chip, the Fn basic is also the Globe

basic. Press the "Globe" button to change to another keyboard (press the "Globe" button repeatedly to rotate in another language or emoji options you lay down for your preferences).

To specify job options (Fn) / land key, open "System Preferences", click "Keyboard", and then select keyboard or source input options, display emojis, and symbols start calling or defining functions. See "Changing Control panel Preferences for Mac" in the macOS user monitor.

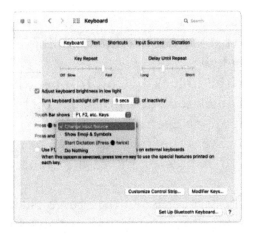

Learn about keyboard shortcuts. You can press a combination of keys to perform tasks on the MacBook Pro that you normally use on a trackpad, mouse, or other devices. For a list of the most commonly used shortcut keys, see the keyboard shortcuts on Mac

MacBook Pro battery charging

As long as the MacBook Pro is connected, the battery in the MacBook Pro will be charged.

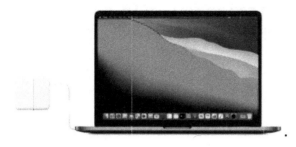

Charge the battery. Use a USB-C charging cable with a 61W power adapter or a 96W power adapter to connect your MacBook Pro to power.

Battery charging is designed to help reduce battery life and extend its service life by learning the daily charging procedures. When expected to be connected to a power supply for a long time, it delays the battery charging time by more than 80% and is designed to charge the battery before discharging the power source. You can change this option in the "Battery" preferences.

You can use any Thunderbolt port to charge your MacBook Pro. When the computer is turned off or in sleep mode, the battery is charging very quickly.

Check battery level. Check the battery status icon on the right side of the menu bar to see the battery level or charging status.

Charging   Charged

Battery usage record. Click battery on system preferences, and then click usage history to view battery usage in the last 24 hours or 10 days.

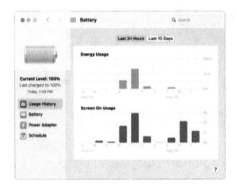

Save battery power. To extend battery life with a given charging time, you can reduce screen brightness, shut down the system and disconnect inactive security devices. Click "Battery" on "System Preferences" to change the power settings. If the MacBook Pro is connected to this device and in sleep mode, the device's battery may run out.

Learn more. For more information:

- For the battery on your Mac, including troubleshooting details, please refer to Apple's support article "About portable Mac batteries"
- How to Monitor Battery on Mac, please refer to "Monitoring the Battery of a Mac Portable Computer" in the macOS User Guide.
- For problems with charging with an adapter, please refer to the Apple Support article: If the USB-C power connector fails to charge your Mac notebook supercomputer, then see "Not Charging" as soon as the Mac notebook computer is connected to a power basis
- For rechargeable internal battery on MacBook Pro, as well as tips for protection and performance, please visit the Apple Lithium-Ion Battery

What to include

To use your MacBook Pro, you need the following two boxed

accessories:

Accessories   meaning

USB-C charging cable: To charge the

MacBook Pro, connect

one side of the USB-C

charging cable to any

Thunderbolt port on a

MacBook Pro, and the

other end to a 61W

power adapter or 96W

power adapter...

AC plug

61W power connector or 96W power

connector:

After connecting the power

connector, fully

extend the power pins to the

AC plug, and then

attach the adapter to the AC

power outlet.

Start MacBook Pro automatically. Connect your 61W power

adapter or 96W power adapter and USB-C charging cable, then lift the lid to turn on and start the MacBook Pro. Sign in and start working.

Some adapters and equipment are sold separately. Please visit Apple.com, your local Apple Store, or other retailers for more information and availability. Check the labels or contact the manufacturer to make sure you select the right product.

Use an external monitor on the MacBook Pro

The Thunderbolt port on MacBook Pro supports video output. You can use an external monitor, projector, or HDTV on your MacBook Pro.

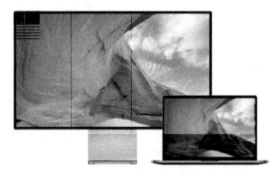

- Connect a VGA monitor or projector: Use a USB-C VGA multi-port adapter to connect a monitor or projector to the Thunderbolt 3 (USB-C) port on a MacBook Pro.
- Connect HDMI or HDTV display: Use a USB-C digital AV multi-port adapter to connect an HDMI or HDTV display to the Thunderbolt 3 (USB-C) port on a MacBook Pro.
- Connect the USB-C controller: Connect the controller to the Thunderbolt 3 (USB-C) port on the MacBook Pro.

Note: The 16-inch MacBook Pro and other 13-inch and 15-inch models can support full 6K resolution on Apple Pro Display XDR. Please refer to the section "System Requirements and Mac Compatibility Models" in the Apple Support article "Setting up and using the Apple Pro Display XDR".

For more information on adapters used to connect external devices, see MacBook Pro Accessories. Adapters and other accessories are sold separately. Please visit Apple.com, your local Apple Store, or other retailers for more information and availability. Check the labels or contact the manufacturer to make sure you select the right product. See Thunderbolt 3 adapter or USB-C port on Mac or iPad Pro.

Tip: When you connect HDTV to an Apple TV, you can use AirPlay to emulate the MacBook Pro screen on a TV screen up to 1080p HD. For more information, see Use AirPlay on Mac.

Learn more. For more information on the extended desktop, video screen, and other preferences, please refer to the Apple Support article Using an external monitor on your Mac. To resolve problems with external monitors, see Getting Help with Video Problems from an external monitor connected to your Mac.

Use wireless accessories

Using Bluetooth® technology, your MacBook Pro can connect wirelessly (that is, pairs) with Bluetooth keyboards, mice, trackpads, headphones, wearable sports accessories, and other devices.

Connect a Bluetooth device. Turn on the device to make it available, then open "System Favorites" and click on "Bluetooth." Select an app from the list and click on "Connect". The device will remain connected until you remove it. Right-click the device name to delete it.

Turn Bluetooth on or off. Click the "Control Center" icon in the menu bar, then click the "Bluetooth" icon, then click the controller to turn on or off Bluetooth. Your MacBook Pro is powered by Bluetooth.

Tip: If you cannot see the Bluetooth icon in the menu bar, you can add it. Click the Bluetooth icon in the Control Center, click

Bluetooth Preferences, and select "Show Bluetooth in the menu bar."

Customize Touch Bar on MacBook Pro

For apps like Finder, Mail, and Safari, you can customize the buttons on the touch bar. You can customize the control bar. Select "View"> "Customize Touch Bar" to add, remove, or rearrange items in Touch Bar.

When you customize the touch bar, the buttons will rotate. For example, this is the "Calculator" touch bar that can be edited:

Insert buttons on the touch bar. Drag controls at the bottom of the screen and enters the touch bar to add them.

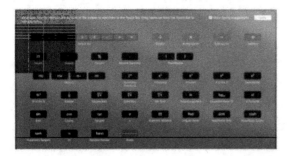

When you are done, click Finish on the screen.

Reset buttons on the touch bar. When customizing Touch Bar, drag the button to a new location. When you are done, click Finish on the screen.

Remove button from touch bar. When customizing the Touch Bar, drag the button from the Touch Bar to the screen to remove it. When you are done, click Finish on the screen.

MacBook Pro trackpad

You can use the simple trackpad touch to do many things on

your MacBook Pro-scroll on the web, zoom in documents, swap photos, etc. With the Force Touch trackpad, the pressure sensor function takes the connection to another level. The trackpad provides feedback — when you drag or rotate objects, you will hear subtle vibrations after alignment, allowing you to work more accurately.

Here are some common actions:

Click the touch icon.

Click: Press anywhere on the touchpad. Or enable "tap to click" on track preferences, and then just tap.

Force the click touch icon.

Force click: Click, then press deep. You can use the power of click to get more information click on a name to see its meaning or click on an address to see a preview that can be opened on the map.

Second click or right touch icon.

Double-click (ie, right-click): Double-click to open the shortcut menu. When "click to click" is enabled, tap with two fingers. On the keyboard, press the control button, and then click the fingerprint clip.

Touchmark of two fingers.

Scroll two fingers: Swipe up or down with two fingers to scroll.

Click to zoom in.

Click to zoom in: Squeeze or open or close your finger to zoom in or zoom out photos and web pages.

Swipe to browse to touch gestures.

Swipe to browse: Swipe left or right with two fingers to browse web pages, documents, etc., as scrolling through pages in a book.

Open the start action icon.

Open launchpad: immediately open the program on the launch-pad. Press four or five fingers, then click the app to open it.

Swipe between app signs.

Swipe between apps: To switch from one full-screen app to another, use three or four fingers to swipe left or right.

Customize your touch. In the system preferences, click the trackpad. You can do the following:

- Learn more about each touch
- Set the click pressure you want to use
- Decide whether you will use the pressure sensor
- Customize some touchpad functions

Tip: If you find yourself forced to click when you don't want to, try adjusting the click-to-click to set it firmly in the "Trackpad" preferences. Or adjust the "Recovery and Data" option from the default "Force tap with One Finger" set to "Three-click".

MacBook Pro Accessories

The following Apple accessories can be used to connect the MacBook Pro to power, external devices, and displays, etc.

USB-C to USB adapter

USB-C on USB adapter: Connect MacBook Pro to standard USB devices.

USB-C cable to Lightning.

USB-C Cable to Lightning: Connect iPhone or other iOS or iPadOS devices to MacBook Pro for synchronization and charging.

Multi-port digital USB-C adapter.

USB-C Digital AV adapter with multiple ports: connect MacBook Pro to HDMI display, and simultaneously connect a standard USB device with USB-C charging cable to charge MacBook Pro.

USB-C VGA adapter for most ports.

USB-C VGA adapter for multiple ports: connect a MacBook Pro to a VGA projector or controller, while connecting a standard USB device with a USB-C charging cable to charge the MacBook Pro.

Thunderbolt 3 (USB-C) adapter to Thunderbolt 2.

Thunderbolt 3 (USB-C) to Thunderbolt 2 adapter: connect MacBook Pro to Thunderbolt 2 device.

Learn more. See the Apple Thunderbolt 3 adapter support article or USB-C port on a Mac or iPad Pro.

Adapters and other accessories are sold separately. Please visit Apple.com, your local Apple Store, or other retailers for more information and availability. Check the labels or contact the manufacturer to make sure you select the right product.

Features of MacBook pro

Design

The M1 MacBook Pro continues to use the same design that Apple has used for many years, with the same rectangular shape, aluminum body, and very small bezels around the display. Mac-Book Pro models are available in silver and gray spaces.

There's a large trackpad, a small hood, a Touch Bar, an Apple logo on the back, two to four ports on the side (depending on the model), and a side speaker grille. The size of the MacBook Pro is 11.97 inches, 8.36 inches wide, and 14.9mm. It weighs three kilograms, which is 0.2 kilograms heavier than the Mac-book Air.

Apple sells a 13-inch MacBook Pro with a large 16-inch model, measuring 14.09 inches long, 9.68 inches wide, and 16.2 mm wide. It weighs 4.3 pounds.

Effective cooling

Inside, there is a new active cooling system designed to keep the MacBook Pro at a lower temperature while the M1 chip works to achieve faster performance.

Display

The 13-inch MacBook Pro model is equipped with a Retina display with 500 nits brightness and supports a wide P3 screen color and True Tone functions. Display resolution is 2560 x 1600 resolution, 227 pixels per inch.

The True Tone feature uses a multi-channel light sensor installed in the new MacBook Pro model, which can determine the brightness and color temperature of the room. After getting a white balance, the MacBook Pro can adjust the color and intensity of the display to match the lighting in the room, leading to natural, paper-like tests, and can also reduce eye fatigue.

Compared to sRBG standard monitors, P3's wide color support has a greater color range and can provide brighter colors.

keyboard

MacBook Pro uses the same keyboard and reusable Microsoft keyboard that was first introduced on the 16-inch MacBook Pro. The Magic Keyboard cancels the butterfly process Apple has been using since 2015 because it is full of key problems that fail due to dust and other small particles.

The scissors on the MacBook Pro keyboard can provide 1mm of key movement and a stable key feel.

The keyboard also has illuminated buttons controlled by a wide light sensor, which can illuminate keys in a dark room.

Touch the bar with the touch ID

All MacBook Pro models have a Touch Bar, which is a small OLED retina multi-touch display built into the keyboard, traditionally where operating keys are available. The touch bar is sensitive to the context and can perform a variety of different functions on a Mac, depending on the application used.

The touch bar is a matte-style display that blends well with other buttons on the keyboard. On all modern MacBook Pro devices, it supports True Tone and can adjust the white balance depending on available lighting conditions.

Collaborate with touch tap, slide, and other multi-touch touches, backing up 10 fingers at a time.

The 13-inch MacBook Pro model also has a Touch ID fingerprint sensor, located next to the touch bar above the keyboard. Touch ID is protected by a security feature, which protects your fingerprints and personal information.

The Touch ID in MacBook Pro can be used instead of a password, while a Mac can be unlocked by placing your finger on the sensor. It can also enter passwords for password-protected applications and can be used to purchase Apple Pay Safari.

Touchpad

The MacBook Pro has a large Force Touch trackpad, no traditional buttons, but a Force Sensors set, which allows users to press anywhere on the trackpad to get the same response.

The magnetic-powered Taptic engine gives users a touchable effect when they use the touchpad, thus instilling the sense of body buttons. The Force Touch trackpad supports light pressure (this is a regular click), and deep press or "force click" (as a separate action), which can complete the function as highlighting the meaning of the word.

the harbor

The 13-inch MacBook Pro entry model with an M1 chip has dual USB-C ports, supports USB 4, and Thunderbolt 3. Its Thunderbolt transmission speed is up to 40Gb / s, and USB transmission speed is up to 10Gb / s. With Thunderbolt 3, the MacBook The Pro model can support a single 6K display at 60Hz.

Apple said the M1 MacBook Pro is limited to one display with a 6K resolution, but with the DisplayPort adapter, the M1 MacBook Air and MacBook Pro models can launch up to five external displays. This is only possible if you are using a 4K and 1080p display mix because the Thunderbolt port does not have the bandwidth to start a 4K display.

The Intel MacBook Pro model has four Thunderbolt ports. Every hole in the MacBook Pro model is the same and can be used for the same function, so the whole port can be used to power the machine. All ports backing the following networks: Power, Thunderbolt, USB, DisplayPort, HDMI, and VGA.

M1 Apple Silicon Chip

The M1 MacBook Pro is the first Mac to use the Arm-based chip designed for Apple instead of the Intel chip as previous models of the MacBook Pro. These chips are named "Apple Silicon", and the chip used on the lesser 13-inch MacBook Pro by 2020 is the M1.

The M1 is the first chip system designed for Apple for Mac, which means it has a processor, GPU, O / O, security features, and RAM, and a chip is installed inside the Mac. Apple said this could provide better performance and energy efficiency, thus increasing battery life.

Like Apple's latest A14 chip, the M1 is made using a 5-nanometer processor, making it smaller and more efficient than Apple's predecessors. It has 16 billion transistors, and Apple claims this is the largest transistor invested in a single chip.

Integrated memory construction

One of M1's functions is integrated memory, UMA, which includes bandwidth, low latency memory. This means that the technology on the M1 chip can access the same data without copying between multiple memory pools, which can greatly improve the performance of the entire system.

Speed development

The M1 has an 8-core CPU and an 8-core GPU integrated (there is also a 7-core GPU option, as described below). The CPU has four very efficient characters and four cores of high performance. When performing simple tasks such as browsing the web or reading emails, the MacBook Pro is equipped with high performance to extend battery life, but for system-enhancing functions such as photo and video editing, high performance is used.

Compared to high-performance cores, efficient cores use one-tenth of power while providing the performance that Mac users need to perform daily tasks.

According to Apple, the CPU speed of the M1 chip is 2.8 times higher than the Intel chip on the previous MacBook Pro, while the GPU speed is seven times higher. Unlike other MacBook Air models with seven GPUs, all M1 MacBook Pro models are equipped with eight GPUs.

Compared to notebook chips, the M1 is designed to provide superior performance in all electrical power. Compared to the latest PC notebook chips, its CPU performance has increased by 2 times, while power consumption has been reduced by 25%.

Xcode building projects speed increased 2.8 times, ProRes code transfer speed in Final Cut Pro increased 2.8 times, multi-core vector performance in Affinity Photo increased 2 times, and Amp Designer plug-supported Logic Pro increased 1.8 times.

Ratings

In the Geekbench bench press test, the 3.2GHz M1 chip has more than 1700 single-core single points and an average of about 7500 backpacks, making it faster than the top 16-inch MacBook Pro models released in 2019. Those 16-inch MacBook Pro models are fitted with the latest Intel tenth chip.

Besides, the one basic functionality offered by the M1 chip is better than any other Mac available. Its performance is better than the Intel-based MacBook Pro models sold for, but GPU performance may not exceed them.

Even if you mimic the x86 under Rosetta 2, the M1 Mac is still faster than all the Macs released earlier. Operating on Apple's Rosetta 2 conversion platform with Geekbench, the Mac can achieve up to 78% to 79% of Apple Silicon code performance.

The benchmark test of the R23 Cinebench M1 chip is 7508 (multi-core) and 1498 (single-core).

In contrast, the 2020 high-end 16-inch 16-inch MacBook Pro with 2.3GHz Core i9 chip received 8818 on multi-core. The single-core score of the low-end 16-inch MacBook Pro at 2.6GHz was 1113, and the multi-core in the same test, the Intel® Core TMTM score is 6912, while the previous generation of high-end MacBook Air has 1119 points and a total of 4329 points.

GPU

The 8-core GPU on the M1 chip is integrated (which means it's not a separate chip), and Apple calls it the world's most integrated graphics on your computers. It can extract 25,000 threads at a time and combine improved graphics performance with lower power consumption.

Apple said the 3D rendering process for the new M1 MacBook Pro has increased by 5.9 times, 3D performance on Shapr3D has increased by 3 times, and performance of the "Shadow Dome" game has also increased by 2.9 times, thanks to the M1 GPU.

In a bench test of GFX Bench 5.0, the M1 beat the GTX 1050 Ti and Radeon RX 560 with a 2.6 TFLOP output.

GPU	Manhattan	T-Rex	ALU 2	Driver Overhead 2	Texturing
Apple M1	407.7 FPS	660.1 FPS	298.1 FPS	245.2 FPS	71,149 MTexels/s
GeForce GTX 1050 TI	288.3 FPS	508.1 FPS	512.6 FPS	218.2 FPS	59,293 MTexels/s
Radeon RX 560	221.0 FPS	482.9 FPS	6275.4 FPS	95.5 FPS	22,8901 MTexels/s

Neural Engine

There is a new, more advanced engine on the MacBook Pro that can increase the speed of machine learning tasks 11 times. The neural engine uses 16 basic configurations, can perform 11 billion tasks per second, and works with machine learning accelerators to perform ML-based tasks faster.

Neural engines can benefit programs such as Final Cut Pro, Pixelmator, and other programs that use video, image, and audio editing.

Active application

The M1 chip is based on the Arm architecture instead of the x96 build as an Intel chip, but thanks to Rosetta 2 (a back-end and invisible user interface), it can still run applications designed for Intel devices.

Apple also encourages developers to build standard applications that use a single binary file and run on Apple Silicon Macs and Intel Macs. Also, Apple Silicon Macs can launch apps designed for the iPhone and iPad.

We provide detailed information about updated apps with traditional or universal help, games on M1 Mac, customization programs, etc. See our M1 tidbits guide for details.

Intel chip

The high-end MacBook Pro models starting at $ 1799 continue to use the 10th generation Intel Core i5 chip. The basic model uses a 2.0GHz quad-core processor, which can be customized on a 2.3GHz quad-core processor. Both Intel models have Intel Iris Plus graphics.

In contrast, Intel's top processors on these machines have 1240 single points and a total of 4517 points, far behind the M1. Most people don't want to buy an Intel-based 13-inch 13. The M1 chip in low-end models is faster, so the MacBook Pro is emerging this time around.

Battery life of M1

With the improved performance of the M1, the battery life of the MacBook Pro is astounding, far surpassing the battery life of the previous generation model.

In the M1 MacBook Pro model, the battery power is 58.2WHr, up to 17 hours when browsing the web, and up to 20 hours when watching movies on the Apple TV app.

Intel-based MacBook Pro models can last up to 10 hours while browsing the web, and up to 10 hours when watching movies on the Apple TV app.

Efficiency test

In an attempt to integrate WebKit's open-source code, Apple's M1 chip performed well. The coding speed of the M1 MacBook Pro and MacBook Air is much faster than similar models based on Intel, but most notably, at the end of testing, the battery life is still 91%, while the battery of a 16-inch MacBook Pro top is 24%. Remaining service life, while the Intel 13-inch MacBook Pro has only 24% battery life.

RAM

The basic M1 model is equipped with 8GB RAM, up to 16GB can be customized. Intel high-end models support up to 32GB of RAM. Experiments have shown that there is no significant difference between the M1 model with 8GB RAM and 16GB RAM, except that there are many system-reinforcing functions to be performed.

SSD

By adding a new SSD controller to the M1 chip, the SSD speed on the M1 MacBook Pro is increased 2 times, and the successive reading speed reaches 3.3GB / s. The M1 MacBook Pro model can be installed up to 2TB SSD with a storage capacity of 256GB, while the Intel model can be equipped with up to 4TB SSD storage.

Communication

The M1 MacBook Pro supports 802.11ax WiFi, which is Wi-Fi 6, which is the latest WiFi. It is faster and more efficient than the previous generation of 802.11ac WiFi, with speeds of up to 1.2Gb / s. It also supports Bluetooth 5.0.

The Intel MacBook Pro is limited to 802.11ac WiFi, also known as WiFi 5.

FaceTime camera and microphone

The 720p HD camera is built into the front of the MacBook Pro for FaceTime phones. Apple has been using the 720p front-facing camera for many years and has not improved image quality, but this year it said the M1 chip could provide clearer and clearer images.

The M1 chip can provide better noise reduction to get more details without shadows and brightness, and the neural engine uses facial detection to correct white balance and exposure to more natural skin tones.

Get started

How to set and customize your Mac from scratch

When you need to move to a new computer, follow the steps below to set up your Mac.

Combining a new Mac (like the new MacBook Air with the M1) is not a bad process. Thanks to iCloud, Mac App Store, and other cloud-based storage providers (like Dropbox), this point is no longer as scary as before. However, when setting up a new laptop from scratch, you still need to make sure you complete some steps.

Here are some footsteps you can take to begin the route of preparation for mediation.

How to set up a Mac

Set up your Mac, Re-authorize your Internet account, Customize your app preferences, Check for software updates, Re-download Mac App Store, Set up your password manager, Customize Finder, Safari, and other app views, Add extensions for Safari for regular sign-in

Step 1: Prepare Mac

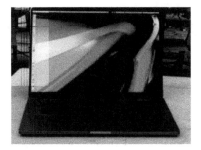

Before you have fun with customizing your Mac, you may have to uninstall and set it up first. Signing into iCloud here will begin the method of syncing the keychain, an online account, and the "Desktop and Documents" folder (if you are working), so it's best to do it right away.

➢ How to set up a fresh Mac

Step 2: Re-authorize your Internet account

Cloud will sync all online accounts on alternative Mac, but any non-Apple accounts must be re-authorized (read: re-enter password) before they can be used again. Therefore, it is best to do the job on a new machine first.

1. Open system preferences.
2. Select the account icon.
3. Click on the account you want to activate, and check the corresponding box (email, message, note, etc.).

Repeat the steps above for each account you want to authorize again.

Step 3: Customize your program preferences

In "System Preferences", you can customize some system features. This consist of but is not boundless to:

- To use black mode in the toolbar (normal)
- Change desktop image and screen saver (desktop and screen saver)
- Your booth size and preferences (Dock)
- FileVault and Gateway (Security and Privacy)
- Notification preferences (notifications)
- How long do you want the monitor to stay in sleep mode (power saving)
- Customizing the touch bar (keyboard)
- Enable calling (keyboard)
- Custom touch (trackpad)
- Alarm sound (sound)
- Open "Return to My Mac" (iCloud, sharing)
- Add more cards to Apple Pay (e-wallet and Apple Pay)
- Customize your app preferences (App Store)
- If necessary, add a VPN (network)
- Pair any Bluetooth accessories, such as headsets (Bluetooth)
- Insert any other fingerprints (Touch ID)
- Enter another user IDs (users and groups)
- Include any restrictions (parental controls)
- Change Siri Preferences (Siri)
- Time Machine Setup (Machine Time)

◦ Add any accessible (accessible)

Step 4: Check for software updates

The new Mac should bring the latest and greatest software, but if you do not use the latest version, you should check for new updates:

1. Go to the Apple list of options in the top left angle.
2. Select "App Store".
3. Click the refresh tab.
4. Install all required updates.

Step 5: Download the Mac App Store app again

Next, you should also download the required Mac App Store apps on the new computer.

1. Go to the Apple list of options in the top left angle.
2. Select "App Store".
3. From any store in the store, click on your profile at the bottom left of the screen. (You may need to sign in to

iCloud all over again.)
4. Download all previously purchased apps you wish to install on your Mac. Check out the download icon.

Step 6: Re-download non-Mac App Store apps

If you use any Adobe products or other non-Mac App Store products, you will not be able to download them again from the App Store: instead, open Safari and download them from their websites. Dropbox is one of the great features: not only is it great to sync folders, but when you use Dropbox to sync information (like 1Password), you need to install it so you can easily access the password.

Step 7: Set up your password manager

In advance, you start customizing Safari with other apps, make sure you can access all of these apps by setting up a keyword manager. (You have a password manager, right? If not, now is a good time to consider using a password manager, so you don't have to worry about passwords when you don't need to set up your device from scratch.)

➢ Excellent Mac password manager app

Step 8: Customize Finder, Safari, and other app views

The "View" menu can completely change the windows of the app to your liking. Custom to-do lists include Finder, Safari, and Mail, but please choose the app you use most often to fix it!

If you have a compatible Mac, this is also the time you would want to customize the touch bar for each program or add "Favorites" to the Mail Toolbar (for some reason, they can't be synced via iCloud).

Step 9: Install Safari Extension

Most of us have used at least one Safari extension on Mac, whether it be a Pinterest modifier, Buffer social, or blocker. After customizing Safari, it's a great time to set up Safari extensions.

- Safari library

Step 10: Log in to frequently used websites

Whether your online addiction includes Facebook, Quora, Twitter, Google, or Reddit, there is a network service you can't live without. Continue to sign in to these codes now, so you don't have to worry about writing code for two things. (You have set two-step authentication, haven't you?)

➤ How to use two-step verification

Step 11: Make sure the post is sent from the correct iCloud address

When you set up your computer from scratch, you will lose a key part of your history: the iMessage archive encrypted and synced only as part of the iCloud backup. Therefore, you need to customize the message settings, including which address to send from default. Otherwise, people may not understand why "icloudjokeaddress@icloud.com" just sent them a message.

Step 12: Log in with music and photos

Want to use Apple Music and the Cloud Photo Library? You need to turn on "Music and Photos" before you can sign in with your Apple ID and password.

Step 13: Enjoy your new Mac!

After completing all the customization, please take the time to enjoy using it! After all, it is fresh and sparkly.

(After that backup, so you do not have to reset from the beginning.)

Apple account on Mac

Apple ID is an account that permits you to use all Apple services. Use your Apple ID to download apps from the App Store; access media in Apple Music, Apple Podcast, Apple TV, and Apple Books; use iCloud to keep content up to date on all devices; set up a family sharing group; and more.

You can also use your Apple ID to access other apps and websites (see "Log in thru Apple on Mac" in the macOS User Monitor).

Important Note: If you forget your Apple ID password, you do not need to create a new Apple ID. Just tap the "Forgot Apple ID or password?" In the login window to recover your password.

If other family members use Apple devices, make sure each family member has their own Apple ID. You can create your child's Apple ID account and share purchases and subscriptions with "Family Sharing", which will be explained later in this section.

To view available Apple ID services, see Where can I use Apple ID?

All in one place. Manage everything related to your Apple ID in one place. Open System Preferences on your MacBook Pro for your Apple ID and Family Sharing settings are on top.

Apple ID window in system preferences. Click items in the sidebar to update your account information, open or close iCloud, manage media accounts, or view all devices signed in with Apple ID.

Update account, security, and payment details. In "System Preferences", click on "Apple ID" and select an item in the sidebar to view and update information associated with your account.

- Overview: The "View All" window lets you know that your account is set up and running; if not, you will see tips and notifications here.
- Name, Phone, Email: Update the name and contact details associated with your Apple ID. You can also manage Apple email subscriptions.
- Password and security: Change your Apple ID password, turn on two-factor authentication, add or remove trusted phone numbers, and create a verification code to sign in to another device or iCloud.com. You can also achieve which apps and websites use "Sign in with Apple". See "Sign in thru Apple" in the macOS user monitor.
- Payment and Delivery: Manage payment methods associated with Apple ID and shipping address from the Apple Store.
- ICloud: Check the checkbox next to the iCloud feature to enable the feature. When you turn on the iCloud feature, your content is stored on iCloud instead of locally on your Mac, so you can access any content on any device that opens iCloud and logs in with the same Apple ID.

- Media and Purchases: Manage accounts associated with Apple Music, Apple Podcast, Apple TV, and Apple Books; select purchase settings; and manage your subscription.

View all your devices. Under the Apple ID sidebar, view all devices connected to Apple ID. You can check if "Find My Device" is open on each device (see "Find My Device"), check the Cloud Backup status of iOS or iPadOS devices, or if you are no longer the owner of the device, start to Remove Device from on account.

Family sharing. By sharing families, you can set up family groups and create Apple ID accounts for your children. To manage your family sharing settings, click on "Family Sharing" in "System Preferences" and select the icon in the sidebar to view and update your details. You can add or remove family members; share media purchases, payment methods, iCloud storage, and location; and set your children's screen time limits (see Screen Time on Mac).

Learn more. To learn more about iCloud and family sharing, see Access iCloud content on Mac and Manage family sharing groups on Mac in the macOS User Guide.

Mac Display Settings

Align the light with the surroundings. Your MacBook Pro is equipped with a Retina display with TrueTone® technology. True Tone will automatically adjust the color of the display to match your natural light to provide a natural viewing experience. In the "Show" window of "System Preferences", turn on or off "Real Tone".

Use a powerful desktop. If you use a powerful desktop image, the desktop image will automatically change to match the time of day in your area. In "System Favorites", click "Desktop and

Screen Saver", then click "Desktop", then select the "Dynamic Desktop" image. To change the screen depending on the time zone, please enable location services. When location services are turned off, the image will change according to the time zone specified in the "Date and Time" preferences

Use the black mode to stay focused. You can use the black desktop scheme, menu bar, Dock, and all built-in MacOS apps. Your content is highlighted in the front and the middle, while the dim controls and windows are back. You see white text in dark background in apps such as "Email", "Contacts", "Calendar" and "Messages", so your vision will be easier when working in a dark place.

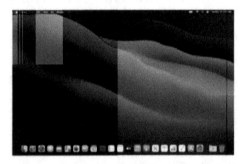

The dark mode is for professionals who edit photos and images - colors and fine details will appear in the background of the black app. Also great for those who just want to focus on their content.

Connect the monitor. See Use the external monitor on MacBook Pro.

Transfer data to the new MacBook Pro

It's easy to move files and settings from any Mac or PC to MacBook Pro. You can transfer data to your MacBook Pro wirelessly or using an Ethernet cable and adapter from Time Machine backup to an old computer or USB storage device.

You may need to upgrade the MacOS version to your old computer before transferring data. Migration Assistant needs

MacOS 10.7 or higher, but it's best to upgrade an old computer to the latest version. If you're not sure if you have a MacBook Pro or want to find out more about other models, please see the Apple Support article "Identify the MacBook Pro Model."

Tip: For best results, make sure your new MacBook Pro uses the latest version of macOS. Open System Preferences and click Software Update to check for updates.

Move from PC to Mac. If you are unfamiliar with Mac and want to transfer from a Windows computer, please refer to the transfer of information from PC to Mac in the macOS user guide and Apple support article Transferring your data from Windows PC to Mac.

Wireless transmission. To transfer data when you set up your MacBook Pro for the first time, use Setup Assistant. To transfer data over time, use the Migration Assistant. Open the Finder window, go to "Applications", open "Applications", and double-click "Migration Assistant" to make wireless migration. Follow the instructions on the screen.

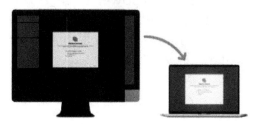

Tip: To transfer data offline from an old computer to a MacBook Pro, make sure both computers are connected to the same network. During the entire migration process, the two computers were close together.

If you use Time Machine to back up files from another Mac to storage (such as an external disk), you can copy files from that device to a MacBook Pro. See Back up and Restore the Mac.

Copy files from USB storage. Use USB-C on a USB adapter to connect a storage device to a MacBook Pro (see MacBook Pro accessories). Then drag the file from the storage device to the Mac-Book Pro.

Use Ethernet transmission. To transfer data via Ethernet, use an adapter (available separately) to connect an Ethernet cable to a MacBook Pro. Connect the other end of the Ethernet cable to another computer (if your computer does not have an Ethernet port, you may need another adapter). Before using Ethernet to transfer data, make sure the MacBook Pro battery is fully charged.

Restore your content. To learn how to restore a Mac from Time Machine or other backups, see the Apple Support Recovery Mac backup article.

Learn more. See the macOS User Guide to transfer data from another computer or device to a Mac, as well as the Apple support article on How to Transfer Content to a New Mac.

Availability on Mac

Your Mac, iOS, and iPadOS devices contain powerful gears that make Apple product features accessible and easy for everyone to use. Mac has four access points to focus on. Click the link to learn more about the features of each location:

- vision
- Hearing
- mobility
- learning

For more information on Apple's accessibility support, please visit Availability.

Accessibility preferences. In the "System Preferences" preferences, "Accessibility" is now set to visual, audio and sports themes, making it easy to find what you need.

Use voice control to complete all tasks. You can only control your Mac with audio. All voice processing voice control is done on the device, so your data will be kept private.

Accurate call. If you cannot enter text by hand, accurate pronunciation is essential for communication. Voice control brings the latest advances in machine learning from speech to text.

You can add custom words to help control the voice to see your frequently used words. Select "System Preferences"> "Accessibility", select "Voice Control", then click "Vocabulary" and enter the words you want. To customize the commands on the Voice Control Preferences page, click Commands and choose to save the default commands or add new commands.

Note: Improved pronunciation accuracy only applies to American English.

Editing rich text. RTF editing commands in voice control allow you to make quick adjustments and then proceed to express your next thought. You can change one phrase to another, quickly set the cursor to edit, and select the text correctly. Try "John has just arrived" as an alternative of "John will be coming soon.". When correcting words, word suggestions and emojis can help you quickly choose what you need.

Perfect navigation. Use voice commands to open and interact with applications. To click on an item, simply specify the name of its accessibility label. You can also say "show number" to see if the number label appears next to all clickable items, then say the number you want to click. If you need to touch the part of the screen without controls, you can say "show grid" to hover the grid on the screen and perform tasks such as clicking, zoom in, drag, etc.

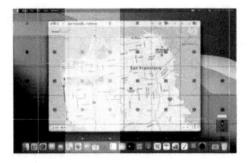

Move up and zoom in. Use the navigation text to display the text's high definition text below the cursor. When you hover your mouse over the text, press the Command button, and a window with enlarged text appears on the screen.

The zoom indicator allows you to zoom in on one monitor, while the other maintains its standard resolution. Watch the same screen closer or closer.

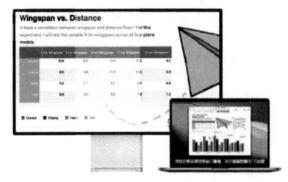

Use VoiceOver Secret. If you like Siri's natural sound, you can choose to use VoiceOver Siri or Speech Siri. Simplified control panel steering requires less drilling in a separate focus group, making it easier to steer with VoiceOver. You can also save custom typing icons on the Cloud and select from the international braille table. Also, if you are an engineer, VoiceOver can now read line numbers, breakpoints, alerts, and errors in the Xcode text editor.

Color enhancement. If you do not see the color correctly, you can use the new color filtering options to adjust the display colors of your Mac. Use the "Accessibility Options" panel to turn on or off your preferences to quickly distinguish colors, and you can access this panel by pressing Touch ID three times.

How to restore Mac to backup

So, you're ready to back up your Mac, but how do you get it back to normal? Here's how to do it right.

You may have heard about backup devices to protect your most valuable data. If you are already using iCloud to sync content, do you need a full backup? Of course, it is. One of the main reasons that a full backup is very important is that it protects you when the device crashes or loses everything.

If you are on a very important and timely project and your Mac fails, you may be able to protect the processed documents in iCloud, but without a backup, your apps or settings will not be protected and it will take a long time to get things back to normal. With the latest backup, you can simply restore your Mac and continue working. Trust me — if you back up your Mac, you'll be much happier.

How to restore Mac to backup:

How to restore Mac to Time Machine backup

If you use Time Machine to back up your Mac, you can restore individual files, or restore the entire hard drive from the most recent backup.

Note: Because you have to install recovery mode on your Mac, it is recommended to print these instructions or switch to another device to read them.

1. Restart Mac.
2. When the boot disc rises, hold the Command and R keys simultaneously. You unlock your Mac in macOS applications. If not, please try again.
3. Select "Restore from Time Machine Backup" from the list of available alternatives.
4. Click Continue.
5. On the System Restore page, click Continue.
6. Choose your Time Machine backup.
7. Click Continue.
8. Select the latest backup for your Mac hard drive. Click Continue.
9. Your Mac will restore the Time Machine backup and restart when finished.

How to restore Mac to local backup

If you back up your Mac with a building program like SuperDuper or Carbon Copy Cloner, you can restore the entire hard drive from the backup, and you can create a boot installer.

Note: Because you have to install recovery mode on your Mac, it is recommended to print these instructions or switch to another device to read them.

1. Restart Mac.
2. When the boot disc rises, hold the Command and R

keys simultaneously. You unlock your Mac in macOS applications. If not, please try again.

3. Click Disk Utility.
4. Click Continue.
5. Select the hard drive for your Mac.
6. Click the "Restore" tab at the top of the Disk Utility window.
7. Select the integrated backup that will be stored on the external hard drive next to "Restore Source".
8. Select the Mac hard drive next to "Restore to"
9. Click Restore.

The Mac will restore the integrated backup and restart when finished.

If you want to install a usable back up, hold the Option button when your Mac restarts, then select Clone from external hard drive to partition hard drive.

How to restore Mac from cloud backup

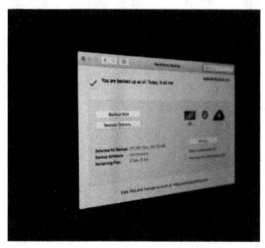

If you use a cloud-based support service (such as Backblaze or CrashPlan), you can download lost data to restore your Mac.

Every cloud-based backup service is different However, every-one needs to download a backup from their remote server - unless the service provides you with a hard physical backup that can be used as a backup (Backblaze provides this feature).

Most programs will provide a "file retrieval" tool on the user interface. You can launch remote applications on your Mac, or visit the company's website.

After that, you can select the files and folders you want to restore from the backup menu.

Because you have to download that file online or send a portable copy, if you do not have a local backup, I only recommend using a cloud-based backup service to restore your Mac. This is time-consuming and less effective than direct recovery from an external hard drive sitting on your desk.

Find your way

Use Finder with Touch Bar in MacBook Pro

Use the touch bar at the top of the keyboard to perform Finder tasks and other tasks.

Use the touch bar. Tap the button to move back and forth between the things you are watching, set view options, and then quickly view, share, or tag items.

Click the "Finder View" button to see the view and edit buttons:

Tap the "Share" button on the touch bar to see sharing options:

Click the label button on the Finder touch bar to see which labels can be used:

Dock on Mac

Dock at the bottom of the screen is an easy place to store programs and documents that you use regularly.

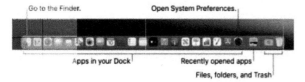

Open the program or file. Click the app icon in Dock, or click the launchpad icon in Dock to view all the apps on your Mac, and then click the app you want. You can also use Spotlight (in the upper right corner of the menu bar) to search for an app, and then open the app directly from Spotlight search results. Recently opened applications will be displayed in the middle section of the Dock.

Close the app. When you click the red dot in the upper left corner of the open window, the window closes, but the app stays open. In Dock, there is a black dot under the open app. To close the application, select "Exit in Application Name" from the application menu (for example, in the "Email" application, select "Exit Email" from the "Email" menu). Or press the Control key and click the Application icon in Dock, then click "Exit".

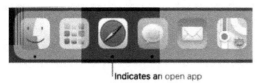

Indicates an open app

Insert the object into Dock. Slog and drop the item at the desired place. Install the application on the left side of the Dock, then insert the file or folder into the appropriate section.

Remove item from the port. Drag and drop out Dock. This item will not be removed from the MacBook Pro, but will only be deleted from the dock.

View all open content on your Mac. Press the control key on the keyboard, or swipe with three fingers on the touchpad to turn on the machine control. View open windows, desktop space, full-screen apps, etc., and easily switch between them. You can also add task control icons to Dock. Please see the Apple Support article Using "Task Control" on Mac.

View all windows open in the app. Force click on the Dakini app to access Exposé and view all open app windows.

Tip: Click Dock and the menu preferences menu to change Dock's appearance and behavior. Zoom in or out of the Document, move it to the left or right of the screen, set it to hide when not in use, and so on.

System Preferences on Mac

System preferences are when you customize your MacBook Pro settings. For instance, use battery favorites to change sleep settings. Or use the "Desktop and Screen Server" preferences to add a desktop image or select screen saver.

Customize your MacBook Pro. Click the "System Favorites" icon in the Dock, or select the "Apple" menu> "System Favorites". Then tap the type of the first choice you want to set. To learn more, see "Modify Mac With System Favorites" in the macOS User Escort.

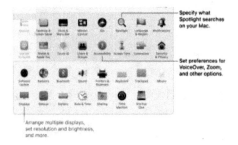

Update macOS. In System Preferences, click Software Update to

Update macOS. In System Preferences, click Software Update to see if your Mac is using the latest version of macOS software. You can specify automatic software update options.

Notification Center on Mac

The notification center has been redesigned to save all significant information, notices, and widgets in a convenient place. Get detailed information on calendar events, stocks, weather, etc., and receive notifications (emails, messages, reminders, etc.) you may have missed.

Open the notification center. Click the date or time in the top right corner of the screen, or use two fingers to swipe left from the right edge of the trackpad. Scroll down to see more.

Share your notifications. Reply to emails, listen to recent podcasts, or view detailed information on calendar events. tap the arrow in the top right corner of the notification to view alternatives, take action, or get more information.

Customize your widget. Click Edit Widgets to add, delete or rearrange widgets. You can also increase third-party widgets from the Mac App Store.

Set your notification preferences. Open System Preferences and tap Notifications to select which notifications you see. Notifications are updated recently, and the redesigned "Modern" widget makes the details clearer.

Desktop, menu bar, and help on Mac

The first thing you see on a MacBook Pro is a desktop supercomputer, where you can swiftly open apps, search anything on the MacBook Pro and the Web, edit files, etc.

Apple menu | The desktop | Finder window | Control Center icon; App menu | Help menu | Menu bar | Wi-Fi icon; Finder icon | System Preferences icon | Dock

Tip: Can't find the screen on the screen? To zoom in a moment, quickly move your finger back and forth on the trackpad. Or, if you use a mouse, slide the mouse back and forth quickly.

Menu bar. The menu bar works at the top of the screen. Use the left-hand menu to select commands and perform tasks in the application. The menu items will change depending on the application you are using. Use the icon on the right to connect to a Wi-Fi network, check your Wi-Fi status icon, open the "Control Center", then click the "Control Center" icon, check that the battery is fully charged, and use Spotlight to search for Spotlight icon, etc.

Tip: You can change the icon displayed in the menu bar. See Control Center on Mac.

Apple Menu. Apple's menu contains frequently used items and is always displayed in the upper left corner of the screen. To open it, tap the Apple sign.

Application menu. You can open multiple applications and windows at once. The name of the active application will be displayed in bold on the right side of the Apple menu, and then the only menu for that application. When you open another application or click an open window in another application, the name of the application menu will change to that application, and the menu item will also change accordingly. If you are looking for a command in the list of options and can't find the command, check the scheme menu to see if the scheme you want is working.

Help menu. Help on MacBook Pro is always available in the menu bar. For help, open the Portal Finder, click the "Help" menu, then select "MacOS Help" to open the macOS User Guide. Or type in the search field and select suggestions. For specific app help, open the app and click "Help" in the menu bar.

For more information, please refer to the macOS User Guide.

Stay organized with stacking. You can use desktops on the desktop to organize files into groups (by category, date, or label) and keep the desktop clean. To view stack content, click the stack to expand its contents, or place the cursor on a stack to view file icons. To create a stack on the desktop, click on desktop and select View> Use Stack or press Control-Command-0. You can also hold the Control key and click on the desktop, then select "Use Stack". To view stack collection options, go to View> Group By, and select an option. After that, all new files you add to the desktop are automatically sorted into the appropriate stack. To learn more, see Organizing files in the file stack on Mac in the macOS User Guide.

Read on to find out about Finder and other desktop features on your Mac.

Spotlight on Mac

The Spotlight Spotlight icon is an easy way to find anything on your MacBook Pro, such as documents, contacts, calendar events, and emails. Exposure suggestions provide information from Wikipedia articles, web search results, news, sports, weather, stocks, movies, and other sources.

Search for anything. Click the Spotlight icon at the top right of the screen and start typing.

Tip: Type Command-Space to show or hide the Spotlight search field.

Change currencies and metrics. Enter the amount (e.g. $, € or ¥) and the value, then press the Return key to get a list of converted prices. Or specify a unit of measurement conversion.

Open the app. Enter the app name in Spotlight and press Return.

Turn off Spotlight suggestions. If you want Spotlight to search only items on your MacBook Pro, open "System Favorites", click "Spotlight", and then click "Siri Suggestions." You can also make some changes to the list of visual search categories.

Siri on Mac

You can talk to Siri on your MacBook Pro, and use your voice to perform many tasks. For example, you can find files, schedule meetings, change preferences, get feedback, send messages, make calls, and add items to your calendar. Siri can rigidity you directives ("How do I get home from here?"), Provide you details ("Just how tall is Mount Whitney?"), Carry out intricate tasks ("make a new menu"), and a lot more.

If you have enabled the "Listen to Hey Siri" "option in Siri preferences, Siri will be available as long as you say" Hello Siri "and immediately state your request.

Note: To use Siri, your Mac needs to be linked to the Internet. Siri may not be presented in all languages or regions, and features may vary by county.

Enable Siri. Open System Favorites, tap Siri, and set options. If Siri is enabled during the setup process, press and hold Command-Spacebar to unlock Siri. Or click Siri on the system preferences, and select Allow to ask Siri. You can set some preferences in the Siri window, such as the language and voice you want to use, and you can show Siri in the menu bar.

Talk to Siri. In the touch control panel, tap the Siri button to turn on Siri, or press and hold the Command-Space bar (or, when you open the feature, say "Hey Siri"), and start talking. By selecting this option in the Siri window of the system preferences, the Siri icon can be added to the menu bar. Then click the Siri icon to apply Siri.

Hello Siri. For MacBook Pro, you just need to say "Hey Siri" to get an answer to your request. To enable this feature in the Siri System Preferences window, click "Listen to Hi Siri" and say a few Siri commands when prompted.

For convenience, when you close the cover of your MacBook Pro, "Hey Siri" does not respond. Once the door is closed and connected to an external monitor, you can still call Siri on the icon in the menu bar.

Tip: To learn more about using Siri, please ask "What can you do?"

Play music. Just say "play music" and Siri does something else. tell Siri: "Play me some popular hip hop songs."

Find and open the file. Let Siri find the files and open them directly from the Siri window. You can ask by file name or description

Drag and drop. Drag and drop a photo and a location from the Siri window into an email, text message, or document. You can duplicate and paste the text.

Change the voice. Click Siri on the system preferences, then selects an option from the Siri voice menu.

In this guide, you'll find Siri suggestions, which look like this:

Ask Siri. Say this:

- "Open the chat of the day I was doing next night"
- "What time is it in Paris?"

Finder on Mac

Use Finder to organize and retrieve files. To open the Finder window, tap the Finder sign in the Dock at the bottom of the display. Force click on the file icon to quickly view its contents, or force click on the file name to edit.

For details on using the Touch Bar for Finder functions, see Use the Finder with Touch Bar on MacBook Pro.

Sync devices. When you connect a device such as an iPhone or iPad, you can see it in the Finder sidebar. From there you can backup, update and restore the device.

Gallery views. Using "Covered passage View", you can see a large preview of the selected file, which gives you a more rapid way to visually view photos, video clips, and other official papers. The preview window displays details to help you identify the file you need. Use the wash bar at the bottom to quickly find what you need. To close or open the preview window, press Shift-Command-P.

Tip: To display the file name in "Gallery View", press Command-J and select "Show Name File".

Take immediate action. In the lower right corner of the "Preview" shortcut window lets you manage and edit files directly in the Finder. You can rotate images into captions, interpret or trim images, combine photos and PDFs into a single file, cut audio and video files, and create custom actions (for example, watermark files) in the Automator workflow.

To show Preview options in Finder, select View> Show Preview. To customize the displayed content, select View> Preview Options, and then select your file type options. See Perform quick actions on Finder on Mac in macOS User Guide.

Tip: choose a file and press the space bar to open "Swift Get". You can sign the PDF; cut audio and video files; then tag, rotate, and crop photos without opening a separate app. To learn more about the "Quick Find" and "Mark" functions, see Use Quick Find view and edit files on Mac and "Mark files on Mac" in the macOS User Guide.

Control Center on Mac

The new "Control Center" integrates the entire menu bar in one place, allowing you to instantly access the most commonly used controls, such as Bluetooth, AirDrop, screenshot, and light and volume control, directly from the menu bar. tap the "Control Center" icon in the top right corner of the display to open the "Control Center".

Click for more options. Click the button to see more options. For example, click the Wi-Fi button to view your preferred network, other networks, or turn on "Network Preferences." To return to the main control center sight, tap the Control Center icon again.

Pin your "Control Center" preferences. Drag your favorite item from the "Control Center" to the menu bar anywhere, so you can easily access it with a single click, open the Quay & Menu Bar Favorites, select the controller on the left, and then tap "Display in Menu Bar" or "Show in Control Center". You will see that the controller will appear at a preview in the menu bar. Some items cannot be added or removed from the control center or menu bar.

Tip: To quickly remove an item from the menu bar, grab the Command key and drag it out of the menu.

Click a feature   Select "Show in Menu Bar"
to view where   to see a feature's location
it appears.   in the menu bar.

The feature's
location is
highlighted in
Control Center

Use MacBook Pro and other devices

How to use screen time on Mac

Time Screen (Mac OS) comes with digital health tools

Like MacOS Catalina, "Screen Time" is now available for Mac for the first time. The tool was launched on iPhone and iPad in 2018 and records the time users spend on various programs from social media to games. It also contains blocking functions to limit usage. There are also parental controls, such as limiting communication, especially for certain contacts. This feature is designed to improve our digital life and sometimes keep it off the screen.

This is how it works.

How to turn on screen time in macOS, how to turn off screen time on macOS, how to share screen time on macOS on all devices, how to add a password to screen time on macOS, how to view app usage during screen time on macOS, how to view notifications send screen time macOS, How to view bakkie during macOS screen, How to set a break time at macOS screen, How to set a time limit on macOS screen, How to set up default allowed content on-screen time MacOS

How to turn on screen time in macOS

The screenshot is still a favorite of the MacOS Catalina program. Start:

1. In "System Favorites", click "Screen Time."
2. choose the "Options" button at the lowest left.
3. tap the "Open" switch in the top right corner.

You can at the moment start using "Display Time" on your Mac.

How to turn off screen time in MacOS

To discontinue using "Display Time" on your Mac:

1. In "System Favorites", click "Screen Time."
2. choose the "Options" button at the lowest left.
3. tap the "Close" switch in the top right corner

How to share screen time in macOS on all devices

To get a more precise picture of how much time you spend online, you can use "Display Time" on all devices. This way, you can view your full-screen time from the app. However, you must first open it.

1. In "System Favorites", click "Screen Time."
2. choose the "Options" button at the lowest left.
3. Tick the share box on all devices.

How to enter a password in `` Screen Time " in MacOS

This way, you can protect your settings and use a password where necessary to extend user usage.

1. In "System Favorites", click "Screen Time."
2. choose the "Options" button at the lowest left.
3. Check the screen-time password usage box.

How to view app usage during screen time on macOS

1. In "System Favorites", click "Screen Time."

2. Select "Application usage" on the left.

On this screen, you can view app usage by day, app, and category. If there are any restrictions (see below), you'll see them here again.

How to view notifications sent during screenshot on macOS

Will receiving daily notifications on your Mac reduce your workload? Want to know who sent all these alerts? Screen time can help.

1. In "System Favorites", click "Screen Time."
2. Select the notification on the left.

View the number of notifications received by whoever receives each day or each week.

How to view capture in `` Screen Time " on macOS

If you want to share "screenshot" information between Apple devices, you can view the number of times the cell phone has been taken by the Mac app. Observing your phone daily can be frustrating.

1. In "System Favorites", click "Screen Time."
2. Select the van on the left.

How to use macOS 'Screen time to schedule downtime

During recess, only the apps you choose to allow can work and make calls (if available). Set downtime schedule:

1. In "System Favorites", click "Screen Time."
2. Choose a break time on the left.
3. Click the Open button to take a break.
4. Use the radio buttons to select daily or customized according to the schedule you want to set.

After selecting "Daily", "Closure" will be forced at the same time each day. After selecting "Custom", you can adjust the time of each day of the week, or uncheck the checkbox next to the day to turn off "Timeoutla "solo day.

How to use macOS screen time to set limits

In Mac "Time Zone", you can set a time limit depending on the app category.

1. In "System Favorites", click "Screen Time."
2. Select application limits on the left.
3. Click the Open button to activate the application limit.
4. Select + to add an application category.
5. Next, check the box next to the apps category you want to limit.
6. As the app section is highlighted, use the radio buttons to set limits. You can set a daily limit or use a custom schedule.
7. Repeat steps 5-6 for each section of the application you want to limit.
8. Click Finish to complete.

Remove app restrictions:

1. In "Mac Screen Time", select "Application Limits" on the left.
2. On the right, uncheck the box next to each application section you no longer want to limit.
3. To turn off app tracking, click the "Close" button.

How to set up pre-screen during macOS

No matter what the other restrictions, you may want the specific process to remain available on your Mac. This may include interactions with specific people or applications.

Set allowable always:

1. In "System Favorites", click "Screen Time."
2. Select "Always Allow" on the left.

3. Check the box next to Always enable everything.

How to Set Content and Privacy with Screen Time for Mac OS

You can also use "Screen Time" to restrict content and privacy.

1. In "System Favorites", click "Screen Time."
2. Select Content and Privacy on the left.
3. Click Open to activate content and privacy.
4. There are four sections here: content, store, app, and more. For each subset, select the checkbox. See the example below.

Access your iCloud content on a Mac

Cloud is an easy way to ensure that all-important content is accessible everywhere. Cloud stores your documents, photos, music, apps, contacts, and calendars, so you can access them whenever you're connected to a network.

You can use your Apple ID to set up a free iCloud account with 5 GB of free storage. The products you purchase in the App Store, Apple TV app, Book Store, or iTunes Store will not depend on your location available.

Cloud keeps everything on your device up to date. So if you have an iPhone, iPad, or iPod touch, just log in to each device with your Apple ID, then open iCloud, and you'll have everything you need.

For system requirements for devices that support iCloud, please refer to the Apple Support Article iCloud Requirements.

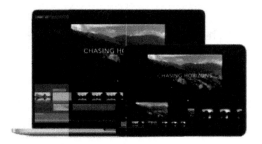

Here are some of the functions you can use in the Cloud.

Automatically save your desktop folder and Text to iCloud Drive. You can save the files in the "Documents" folder or on your desktop, and they will be automatically available on Cloud Drive and can be found anywhere. If you use iCloud Drive, you can access files on your MacBook Pro, the "Files" app on your iPhone or iPad, iCloud.com on the web, or your Windows PC in the iCloud app. When you make changes to your file or Cloud Drive, you can see the changes wherever you look.

First, open "System Preferences", click on "Apple ID", then click on "iCloud". Select "Cloud Drive", then click "Options", then select "Desktop Folders and Documents." To learn more, see Apple's support article "Adding Desktop and Document Files to Cloud Drive".

Share shopping and storage and family sharing. Up to six family members can share items purchased from the App Store, the Apple TV app, the Book Store, and the iTunes Store, and share the same storage plan, even if each of them uses his or her iCloud account. Use a credit card to pay for family purchases, and allow child use directly from a MacBook Pro, iOS device, or iPadOS device. You can share photos, family calendars, reminders, and places. If you did not set home sharing when setting up your Mac, open System Preferences, click Home Sharing, and then click Next to learn more, see the Apple Support article "Set Up Family Sharing."

Use iCloud Photos and Shared Albums to store and share photos. Store photos in iCloud, then view photos and videos and edit them on all devices. Only share photos and videos with the people you choose, and let them add their photos, videos, and comments. First, open "System

Favorites", click "Apple ID", then click "iCloud", then select "Photos." To learn more, see the Apple support article "Setting and using iCloud Photos."

Enjoy shopping everywhere. After signing in to a device with the same Apple ID, no matter what computer or device you use, you can always shop in the App Store, Apple TV application, Book Store, and iTunes Store. Buy them. So, wherever you are, you can use all the music, movies, books, etc.

Use "Find My Mac" to find your MacBook Pro. If your MacBook Pro is lost, you can use Find My Mac to find it on a map, lock its screen, and erase its details remotely when you open "Find My Mac". To open "Find My Mac", open "System Favorites", click "Apple ID", click "iCloud", and then select "Find My Mac". Please check the Apple Support article if Mac yours is lost or stolen.

Note: If your MacBook Pro has multiple user accounts, only one can open "Find My Mac".

Use conversion on Mac

With "Handover", you can continue on one device without using it on another. Process the presentation on the MacBook Pro, then continue on the iPad. Or start an email on iPhone, and complete email on MacBook Pro. View the message on the Apple Watch, then reply to the MacBook Pro. You do not have to worry about transferring files. When the MacBook Pro and device are close, as long as operations are possible, an icon will appear in the dock. To continue, simply tap on the logo.

Note: To use Handoff, you require an iPhone or iPod touch with iOS 8 or later, or an iPad with iPadOS. Make sure the MacBook Pro, iOS device, or iPadOS device has Wi-Fi and Bluetooth turned on, and log in with the same Apple ID.

Open Handoff on MacBook Pro. Open "System Preferences", click "General", then select "Allow switching between this Mac and iCloud device"

Open "Switch" on your iOS or iPadOS device. Go to "Settings"> "General"> "Change" and tap to open "Toggle". If you do not see this option, your device does not support switching.

Open "Convert" to Apple Watch. In the Apple Watch app on your iPhone, go to "Settings"> "General" and tap to enable "Allow conversion".

The switch function works in Safari, email, calendar, contacts, maps, messages, notes, reminders, key expressions, numbers, and pages.

Use MacBook Pro with iCloud and Continuity

There are many ways to use MacBook Pro with iPhone, iPad, iPod touch, or Apple Watch. You can transfer files, share and edit documents, use Apple Watch to open MacBook Pro, convert iPhone or iPad into an Internet hotspot, answer calls or send texts via MacBook Pro, etc.

Access your content across devices. With iCloud, you can securely store, organize, and share documents, photos, and videos on all devices to ensure they stay up to date. To get started, see Right to use your iCloud content on Mac.

If you did not turn on iCloud when you set up your Mac for the first time, please open "System Favorites", click "Sign In", and sign in with your Apple ID. If not, please create a new Apple ID. Click iCloud, then open or close the iCloud function. For more information, please refer to Setting iCloud on Mac in the macOS User Guide.

Use MacBook Pro and other devices. You can use Continuous seamless switching between MacBook Pro and other devices. Just use your Apple ID to sign in on each device, and whenever the MacBook Pro and device are close, they can easily interact. You can start work on one device, then complete work on another device (see "Use Switch" on Mac), copy and paste between devices (see "Use Universal Clipboard" on Mac), answer calls or send texts from MacBook Pro (see calls) and SMS on Mac), use AirDrop to transfer files (see Use AirDrop on Mac), etc. For more placement details, see the following sections.

For a list of program requirements for Supporting Devices, please refer to the Apple Support Article Process System Requirements for Mac, iPhone, iPad, iPod touch, and Apple Watch. To learn more about using Continuity on MacBook Pro, please refer to the Apple support article "Connecting Mac, iPhone, iPad, iPod touch and Apple Watch with Continuity", or go to all devices.

Use Universal Clipboard on Mac

Copy content from one device and paste it to another nearby device in a short time. Content on the sticker board is transmitted via Wi-Fi and can be used on all Mac, iPhone, iPad, and iPod touch devices logged in with the same Apple ID and enable Handoff, Wi-Fi, and Bluetooth. See Use handoff on Mac.

Note: To use General Clipboard, you require an iPhone or iPod touch with iOS 10 or later, or an iPad with iPadOS.

Apply to all applications. You can copy and paste photos, text, photos, and videos among any apps that support copying and pasting on Mac, iPhone, iPad, and iPod touch.

Copy and paste the files. You can use the universal paste board to quickly move files from one Mac to another. Copy files to MacBook Pro and paste them into the Finder window, email message, or any other application in nearby apps that support copying and pasting. On both Macs, you must sign in with the same Apple ID.

Sidecar on Mac

With Sidecar, you can turn your iPad into a second show for your Mac. Give yourself more work space, draw with Apple Pencil, mark PDFs, and screenshots, etc.

Memo: You can use Sidecar with iPad prototypes that support Apple Pencil and use iPadOS 13 (or higher). For more information, see the Apple Support Pics link for the Apple Pencil on the iPad and use the iPad as a second display for Mac and Sidecar.

Connect your iPad. Click the "Control Center" icon in the menu bar to open the "Control Center", click the "Screen Mirroring" icon, and select your iPad. After enabling Sidecar, the icon will turn into a blue iPad. To disconnect the iPad on Mac, open the AirPlay menu and select Disconnect. You can also disconnect by clicking the "Disconnect" icon in the iPad sidebar.

Tip: If you do not see the iPad in the AirPlay menu, please ensure that the Wi-Fi or Bluetooth function of the iPad is turned on. You also need to sign in with the same Apple ID on both devices.

Wired or wireless. Connect the iPad with a cable and keep it charged, or use the iPad wirelessly within 10 meters of Mac.

Extend your desktop. When you connect an iPad, it will automatically become a desktop extension for Mac. To get started, simply drag your apps and documents to the iPad.

The screen of your desktop. To show the Mac screen on both devices, open "Monitor Mirroring" in the "Control Center" and select "Mirror the retina show". To expand the desktop again, open the menu and select "Use as a separate monitor."

Use the Apple Pencil. Directly design and create technology applications of your choice. Just drag the window from Mac to iPad and start using Apple Pencil. Or use Apple Pencil to mark PDFs, screenshots, and photos. To learn more, see Continuity Sketch and Continuity Markup on Mac.

Note: The pressure and inclination of the Apple Pencil are only allowed for applications with advanced pen support.

Use sidebar shortcuts. Use the sidebar on the iPad to quickly access frequently used buttons and controls. Press the button to undo the operation, use the keyboard shortcuts and show or hide the menu bar, Dock, and keyboard.

Use touch bar controls. For apps with Touch Bar support, controls will be displayed at the bottom of the iPad display.

Set preferences. To set Sidecar preferences, open "System Preferences" and click on "Sidecar". Or select "Sidecar Preferences" from the "Screen Mirroring" menu in the Control Center. You can specify the device you want to connect to, change the sidebar and touch the bar on the iPad, and double-tap with the Apple Pencil for quick access to tools.

Camera continuity on Mac

Use an iPhone, iPad, or iPod touch to scan a document or take a close-up photo, and it will instantly appear on your Mac. Many applications support Continuity Camera, including Finder, Email, Messages, etc.

Note: To use the continuous camera, you need an iPhone or iPod touch with iOS 12 (or higher) or an iPad with iPadOS 13 (or higher). Make sure your MacBook Pro and iOS or iPadOS devices have Wi-Fi and Bluetooth turned on and sign in with the same Apple ID.

Insert an image or scan. For applications such as "Email", "Notes" or "Messages", click the location of the photo you want, select "File (or insert)"> "Import from iPhone or iPad", select "Take Photo" or "Scan Document" and take a photo or scan a photo on your iOS or iPadOS device. Before taking a photo, you may need to select an iOS or iPadOS device. Click Apply Image or continue scanning. If you want to try again, you can also click Restart.

In a page-like application, click where you want to insert the image, then press the control button and click, select "Import image", and take a picture. Before taking a photo, you may need to select a device.

Note: To scan on an iOS or iPadOS device, drag the frame until the content to be displayed appears in the frame, then click "Save Scan" and "Save" respectively. Click Restart to re-scan the content.

The image or scan appears in the desired location in the document.

Continuation drawings and progression marks on Mac

With continuous drawing, you can use an iPhone or iPad nearby to draw drawings and instantly upload them to documents on your Mac, for example, emails, messages, documents, or notes. Or use "Continuous Symbols" to edit a document with your finger on an iOS device or Apple Pencil on an iPad, and view these tags on a Mac.

Note: To use Continuity Sketch and Continuity Markup, you need an iPhone or iPod touch with iOS 13 (or higher) or an iPad with iPadOS 13 (or higher). Make sure your MacBook Pro and iOS or iPadOS devices have Wi-Fi and Bluetooth turned on and sign in with the same Apple ID. Apple Pencil Pressure and Tilt only apply to apps with the help of advanced writing.

Insert drawing. For applications such as mail, notes, or messages, place the cursor where you want to insert the drawing. Hand-picked "File (or Install)"> "Import from iPhone or iPad", then select "Install Sketch". On an iOS or iPad device, use your finger or the Apple Pencil (on the iPad supporting the iPad) to draw a drawing, then click on "Finish". On a Mac, a drawing appears where the cursor is located. Depending on where you place the drawing, you can mark it or adjust other features, such as enlargement.

Mark the text. For continuous tagging, you can use the nearest iPad icon or the iPhone / iPod touch iPhone icon to mark PDFs, screenshots and photos, and view the results on your Mac. Press and hold the space bar to view the document immediately, then click the device icon. When both devices are close, click the "Define iPad Tag" icon and select the device. The tool can be highlighted to show that your device is connected.

Use your finger or the Apple Pencil (on iPads that support this feature) to start writing, drawing, or adding shapes. When updating on iPad, iPhone, or iPod touch, you can check for real-time updates on Mac.

Phone calls and text messages on Mac

You can answer and make calls directly from your MacBook Pro. You can receive and send an SMS.

Note: To make or receive calls on MacBook Pro, a Wi-Fi connection is required.

Set up FaceTime for the phone. For iPhone, go to "Settings">

"Phone" and enable Wi-Fi hits on iPhone (iOS 9 or later). After that, on your Mac, go to FaceTime> "Preferences", select "Settings", and then click "Call from iPhone". See the Apple support article "Set iPhone and Mac to make calls."

Answer or make calls. When someone calls your iPhone, click the notification displayed on the MacBook Pro screen. If you do not install headphones, your MacBook Pro becomes a hands-free phone. To make a call on a Mac, open FaceTime and enter a phone number. Or, in "Contacts", click the phone icon in the FaceTime line as a contact. You can also click on the phone number in Spotlight search or in apps such as Safari or Calendar (iPhone or iPad with mobile connections should be nearby) Please refer to the "FaceTime User Guide" to make a call from the Mac app.

Part of the Mac screen showing the call notification window.

Tip: Temporarily turn off notifications about calls, messages, etc. On your Mac, please turn on the "Do Not Disturb" feature. Click the "Control Center" icon in the menu bar, then click "Do Not Disturb" and select a time limit.

Send and receive messages. Use iMessage to send unlimited messages to friends using Macs, iOS devices, iPadOS, and Apple Watch devices. Send and receive SMS or MMS text messages directly from MacBook Pro. When friends and family send messages to you, you can use a nearby device to reply. All messages will appear on MacBook Pro, iPhone, iPad, iPod touch, and Apple Watch. See message.

Fast hotspot on Mac

Lost Wi-Fi connection? With Instant Hotspot, you can use a Personal Hotspot on your iPhone or iPad to connect your MacBook Pro to the Internet instantly - without a password.

Note: "Personal Hotspot" requires iPhone with iOS 8 (or higher) or iPad mobile with iPadOS 13 (or higher). Please refer to

Apple's backing article "How to set up an own hotspot on iPhone or iPad"

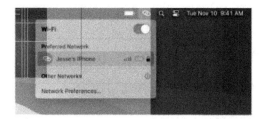

Connect to the device's hotspot. Click the Wi-Fi status icon in the menu bar, then click the link icon next to the iPhone or iPad list (if you don't see the list, click another network). The Wi-Fi icon in the toolbar changes to the "link" icon. You do not need to do anything on the device — the MacBook Pro will automatically connect.

Tip: If you are asked to enter a password, make sure the device is set correctly. See Apple's backing article "Using Instant Hotspot" to connect to your "Personal Hotspot" without entering a keyword.

Check the connection status. Check the Wi-Fi status menu for mobile signal strength.

If you do not use the hotspot, the MacBook Pro will disconnect to save battery life.

Use AirDrop for Mac

With AirDrop, you can easily share files and devices on nearby Mac, iPhone, iPad, and iPod. These devices do not need to share the same Apple ID.

Note: AirDrop for iOS or iPadOS requires a device with a Lightning or USB-C connector with iOS 7 (or higher) or iPadOS 13 (or higher). Not all older Macs back AirDrop (for a list of sustained Macs, see the Apple support article "Using AirDrop on Mac").
The AirDrop Finder window is selected in the "Favorites" section in the sidebar.

Send files from Finder. Hold the Control key and click the item you want to send, select "Share"> "AirDrop", and select the device you want to send to. Or click the Finder icon in the Dock, and click the AirDrop in the left-hand bar (or select "Go"> "Air-Drop"). When someone wants to send a file from a window, drag the file from the desktop or another Finder window into them. When you send a file to someone, the recipient can choose whether to accept that file.

Send files from the app. If you are using an application such as "Page" or "Preview", click the "Share" button and select "Air-Drop", then select the device you want to send to.

Control who can use AirDrop to send you emails. Click the "Control Center" icon in the menu bar, click "AirDrop", and then select "Contacts Only" or "Everyone". You can turn on and off AirDrop here. The iPad, iPhone, and iPod touch have similar settings. Please refer to Apple's support article "How to adjust Air-Drop settings".

Tip: If you cannot see the recipient in the AirDrop window, please make sure both devices have AirDrop and Bluetooth turned on and are 9 meters from each other. If the recipient is using an older Mac, try clicking on "Can't find the person you're looking for?".

Use AirDrop to find items. When someone uses AirDrop to send you something on your Mac, you can choose to receive and save it. If you see an AirDrop notification and need an item, click "Accept" and choose to save it in the "Downloads" folder or an application similar to "Photos". If you use the same iCloud account to access multiple devices, you can easily send an item (for example, a photo from an iPhone) from one device to another and save it automatically.

Share the password stored on the iCloud key. In Safari, you can use AirDrop to share account keywords with a contact or a different Mac, iPhone, iPad, or iPod touch. From the Safari menu, open "Preferences"> "Passwords", select the website you want to share your password with, and hold the Ctrl key and click. choose"Share AirDrop", then choose the person or device in the AirDrop window to share the secret code.

Learn more. See Use AirDrop on Mac to send files to a device near you in the MacOS user guide, and Apple support article Use Air-Drop on Mac.

How to set up and manage Apple Pay on Mac

Apple Pay is an easy and secure way to pay when you use a Mac to buy goods online. Here's how to set it up!

iPhone, Apple Watch, and Mac all backing Apple Pay. Whether you're using the new MacBook Air, the MacBook Pro with Touch Bar, or quiet using the old Mac, here's how to set up Apple Pay and manage your e-wallet.

How to set up Apple Pay on Mac

Before you can use Apple Pay on Mac, you need to set it up.

1. Open Safari on Mac.
2. Click Safari in the top left corner of the Mac.
3. Click System Preferences.

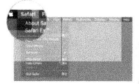

4. Click the "Privacy" tab.
5. Check the boxes next to Apple Pay and Apple Card to let websites inform you of payment options.

Set up Apple Pay on MacBook Air or MacBook Pro with Touch Bar

If you have a MacBook Air or a MacBook Pro with Touch ID, you can authorize direct payments from the keyboard. But before you can do that, you need to install a credit card in Apple Pay. If you set up your Mac for the first time, you will be notified that you have done so, but you can still set up Apple Pay at any time with the System Preferences app.

1. Open system preferences.
2. Click on the e-wallet and Apple Pay icon.

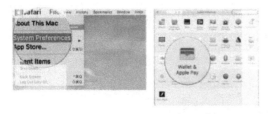

3. Press the Add Card button to add a new credit or bank card.

4. You can place the card in front of the iSight camera to read its number automatically, or you can enter the card details yourself.

5. Click Next to confirm your card number.
6. Verify the card time and enter a three-digit security code.
7. Click Next.

8. Click Accept to accept your card terms and conditions.
9. Choose a verification method to verify card settings.
10.   Click Next.

11. Enter the verification code sent to you in the way you choose.
12. Click Next.

Your card will now be credited to Apple Pay. If this does not happen immediately, your bank may take longer to verify your details. In this case, you will be notified if your information is approved or if further action is required.

If you need to change or delete your Apple Pay card, you can do so in the "System Preferences" program at any time.

Set up Apple Pay on older Macs

If you are using an older Mac, you need to use a memory card for your iPhone or Apple Watch to pay for goods and services.

1. Launch the "Settings" app.
2. Tap on "Wallet" and "Apple Pay".
3. Slide the "On / Off" button next to "Allow Payments" on your Mac in the "On" area.

How to use Apple Pay on Mac

If you buy mostly online on your Mac, Apple Pay lets you pay on your Mac using the Touch ID (or Face ID) sensor on your MacBook Air, MacBook Pro, or iPhone or with Apple's approval Watch, don't say, say on Ara, type your credit card information everywhere that you need it. This is a way to use Apple Pay to pay for goods on Mac!

> ➤ How to use Apple Pay on Mac

How to manage an Apple Pay card on a Mac

After inserting the card into the Mac that supports Touch ID, you can view it in detail in the "Wallet and Apple Pay" section of "System Preferences".

1. Open "System Preferences" on Mac that supports Touch ID.
2. Click on the e-wallet and Apple Pay icon.

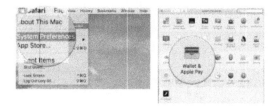

3. To view card details (including your device's account number, billing address, banking contact details, and transactions), select the sidebar.

If you are using Apple Pay with an older version of Mac for an iPhone or Apple Watch, you should carry a card on the iPhone.

How to change your default card

If you add more than one card, you can change it on the Favorites screen.

1. Open "System Preferences" on Mac that supports Touch ID.
2. Click on the e-wallet and Apple Pay icon.

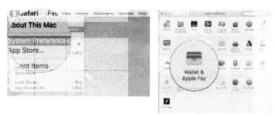

3. At the bottom of the screen, select the card you want

to use as the default option from the drop-down menu.

How to remove the card

1. Open "System Preferences" on Mac that supports Touch ID.
2. Click on the e-wallet and Apple Pay icon.

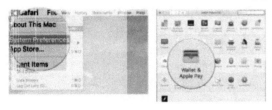

3. Select the card you want to remove from the sidebar.
4. Press the button ((remove) at the bottom of the side-bar.
5. Make sure you want to remove the card.

How to manage your contact and posting details

You can view and change current contact information (shipping address, email, and phone number) in the settings screen.

1. Open "System Preferences" on Mac that supports Touch ID.
2. Click on the e-wallet and Apple Pay icon.

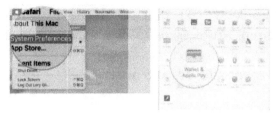

3. Select the "Communication and Distribution" option at the bottom of the sidebar.

To change your shipping address, email, or phone number, please select the option you want to set as the default drop-down menu. You can also add a new address, email, or phone number here.

How to manage your billing address

If you want to change the billing address, you can do so by selecting the query card.

1. Open "System Preferences" on Mac that supports Touch ID.
2. Click on the "Wallet and Apple Pay" icon

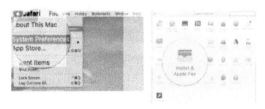

3. Select the card you want to replace from the sidebar.
4. Under the "Payment Address" drop-down menu, select "Add New Payment Address."
5. Enter a new payment address and press Save.

How to look at the latest Apple Pay transactions

Want to check out the latest purchases with your Apple Pay card? You can do this on the "System Favorites" display.

Note: If you want to see what was done recently with the Apple Card, you should watch what is being done on your iPhone.

1. Open "System Preferences" on Mac that supports Touch ID.
2. Click on the e-wallet and Apple Pay icon.

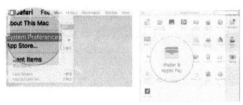

3. Select the card you want to view from the sidebar.
4. Click the transaction tab at the top of the screen.

For your Mac to remind you of all transactions made on your Mac using this card, you can also check the display notification displays from the card check box.

How to return an item using Apple Pay

Each vendor policy is different; some features can be removed with the click of a button, while other features may require you to use Touch ID to re-authorize or return to the store.

How to Solve Apple Pay

If you can't get Apple Pay to accept your card, the easiest solution is to try entering your details again. In the worst-case scenario, you may need to call a debit card. For example, the card we were trying to set up never sent a verification code to the phone number in this file, so we had to get it manually by phone.

Use AirPlay for Mac

Use AirPlay screen view to show everything on the MacBook Pro on the big screen. To emulate the MacBook Pro display on a TV screen or to use HDTV as a second display, connect your HDTV to Apple TV and make sure Apple TV and MacBook Pro are on the same Wi-Fi network. You can also play online videos directly on HDTV without displaying the content on the desktop, which allows you more if you want to play a movie but not in public.

Use the screen display to emulate your desktop. Click the "Control Center" icon in the menu bar, click "Screen mirroring", and then click on "Apple TV". When AirPlay is enabled, the icon becomes blue.

Note: If your Mac supports the AirPlay screen view, when Apple TV and Mac are on the same network, you will see an AirPlay status icon in the menu bar of your Mac. See Use AirPlay play video or mimic the device screen.

In some cases, you can use AirPlay displays even if the MacBook Pro and Apple TV are not on the same Wi-Fi network (also known as AirPlay peer-to-peer). To use Peer-to-Peer AirPlay, you need an Apple TV (third generation rev A, model A1469 or higher) with Apple TV software 7.0 or higher.

Play web videos without showing off the desktop. When you find a web video with an AirPlay icon, click on the icon, then select your Apple TV.

Tip: If the image does not fit your HDTV screen when viewing the screen, please adjust the desktop size to get the best picture. Click the AirPlay icon in the video and select the option under "Match Desktop Size".

Apple TV is sold separately at Apple.com or your local Apple Store.

Learn more. To learn more about AirPlay, see "Use AirPlay to stream content on your Mac to HDTV" in the macOS user guide. To learn more about using the second display on the MacBook Pro, see Using the external display on the MacBook Pro. To resolve the issue, please refer to the Apple support article If Air-Play or Screen Mirroring is not available on your device.

Use AirPrint on Mac

You can use AirPrint wireless to print at:

- Printers are powered by AirPrint on Wi-Fi networks
- Network printer or shared printer for another Mac over Wi-Fi network
- The printer is connected to the USB port of the AirPort base station

Print and print for AirPrint. When you print from the app, click on the "Printer" menu from the "Print" dialog box, then select the printer from the "Nearby Printers" list.

Can't find the printer you want? Make sure you connect it to the same Wi-Fi network as the MacBook Pro. If you are connected but still do not see it, try adding it: open System Preferences, click Printers & Scanners and click the Apply button. (You may need to use a USB cable and adapter (if necessary, temporarily connect the printer to the MacBook Pro).)

Learn more. See wireless printing from Mac to AirPrint printer in macOS Guide.

Unlock Mac and enable Apple Watch activities

If you are wearing an Apple Watch, you can use it to unravel your MacBook Pro and enable verification features such as entering a password, unlocking notes and preferences, and authorizing installation without entering a password. These features use strong encryption to provide a secure connection between Apple Watch and MacBook Pro.

To use the automatic turn-on and enable Apple Watch feature, please do the following:

- Use the same Apple ID to log in to the Mac and Apple

Watch.
- Make sure your Apple Watch is turned on and use watchOS 3 or higher to automatically unlock your Mac; watchOS 6 or higher is required to approve the authentication request.
- Turn on two-factor authentication (see below).

Set up two-factor authentication in your Apple ID. To turn on two-factor authentication, go to Apple> "System Preferences"> "Apple ID"> "Password and Security" and select "Set up two-factor authentication." Please refer to the Apple support article Two-factor authentication for Apple ID.

Make sure that "Disable automatic login" is also selected. (When using FileVault, you will not see this option, but you can still use the functions of "Auto Unlock" and "Approve via Apple Watch".

Set to open automatically. Use the same Apple ID to log in to all devices, and then open "System Preferences" on the MacBook Pro. If your Apple Watch has watchOS 6 installed, click "Security and Privacy", then click "General", and then select "Use Apple Watch to unlock apps with Mac". If your Apple Watch has watchOS 3 to watchOS 5 installed, please select "Allow Apple Watch to unlock Mac". Unless you have watchOS 6 or higher, you cannot authorize authentication activities.

Note: These functions are only available if your Apple Watch has been verified by the login code. Verification is required every time the Apple Watch is installed, so there is no need to perform other steps after entering the password.

Skip login. Put the Apple Watch on your wrist and go to sleep, then lift the protective cover or press the key to wake up the MacBook Pro-Apple Watch unlocks it, so you can work.

Approve the use of the Apple Watch. When you are prompted to enter the password, double-click the separate button on the Apple Watch to confirm the password on the Mac. You can view passwords in Safari, allow installation of apps, unlock locked notes, etc. (watchOS 6 is required).

learn more. Please refer to the macOS User Guide to turn on your Mac and approve applications with Apple Watch.

New features on your MacBook Pro

Design

The design of the 16-inch MacBook Pro is similar to that of the previous 13th MacBook Pro, but the body is slightly larger, the frame is smaller and larger than the 13-inch model also sold by Apple.

From a design point of view, compared to previous MacBook Pro models, the 16-inch MacBook Pro looks no different. It continues to have the same common building features, including a large trackpad, a small hinge, a Touch Bar, and an Apple logo. background., Side speakers and silver and gray options.

The 16-inch MacBook Pro measures 14.09 inches long, 9.68 inches wide, and 16.2 mm wide. It weighs 4.3 pounds. Compared to the 15-inch MacBook Pro, it is bigger, heavier, and bigger.

The 15-inch MacBook Pro measures 13.75 inches long, 9.48 inches wide, and 15.5 mm wide. It weighs about 15 pounds [4 kg].

Show off

The 16-inch MacBook Pro features a Retina display with 500 light signals, wide P3 screen color support, and Tone Tone function.

True Tone uses a bright multi-channel light sensor installed on the new MacBook Pro model, which can determine the brightness and color temperature of the room. After getting a white balance, the MacBook Pro can adjust the color and intensity of the display to match the lighting in the room, leading to natural, paper-like tests, and can also reduce eye fatigue.

The 16-inch MacBook Pro display has a traditional resolution of 3072 x 1920 by 226 pixels per inch (advanced over a 15-inch MacBook Pro).

The 16-inch MacBook Pro has a flexible upgrade, which can be set to the standard of the edited or viewed video frame. Options include 47.95, 48, 50, 59.94, and 60Hz.

keyboard

The 2019 16-inch MacBook Pro is the first Mac to be restructured with the new "Magic Keyboard", which calls off the way the butterfly Apple has been using since 2015. Apple said this will provide users with a "very good typing experience." Mac laptop. "

The butterfly machine is unpopular among customers due to

the tendency of dust and other small particles to create major failures, and due to the new scissors switch keyboard installed on the 13-inch MacBook Pro, the butterfly method has been removed.

According to Apple, the scissors-based approach to the universal keyboard provides 1mm of key movement and a stable key feel, combined with Apple's dome-made rubber dome, designed to store more power to make buttons respond.

Apple said the Magic Keyboard can provide a comfortable, satisfying and quiet typing experience. From a design perspective, the keyboard is similar to the previous keyboard, but there is a portable escape key in the touch bar instead of the visible key, and the Touch ID button is also a different button.

The arrow keys have been rearranged, and the modified layout made by the arrow keys is different from the previous MacBook Pro keyboard design. The touch bar is also slightly away from the keyboard keys.

Apple still offers keyboard service programs on all MacBook, MacBook Air, and MacBook Pro with butterfly keyboards, including the 2019 MacBook Pro models in May 2019 and July 2019. The keyboard service system does not work on a 16-inch MacBook Pro or 2020 13-inch MacBook Pro because they use a newer and more reliable method.

Touch pad

Like previous models of the MacBook Pro, the 16-inch MacBook Pro is equipped with a large Force Touch trackpad that sits mostly on the bottom of the machine.

The Force Touch trackpad does not have traditional buttons but is enabled by a set of "force sensors", which allows the user to press anywhere on the trackpad to get the same response. The Taptic drag-operated engine provides users with a touchable response when using the touch pad, thus instilling the feeling of body buttons.

The Force Touch trackpad supports light pressure (this is a regular click), and deep pressure or "force force" (as a separate action), which can complete tasks such as highlighting the meaning of a word.

Touch bar

There's a Touch Bar on the 16-inch MacBook Pro, which is a small OLED Retina that shows a multi-touch built-in keyboard, traditionally where operating keys are located.

Touch Bar is sensitive to context and can perform a variety of functions on a Mac, depending on the system used, and is now available throughout the Apple MacBook Pro series.

The touch bar is a matte-style display that blends well with other buttons on the keyboard. On all modern MacBook Pro devices, it supports True Tone and can adjust the white balance depending on available lighting conditions.

Collaborate with touch tap, slide, and other multi-touch touches, backing up 10 fingers at a time.

In 2019, Apple upgraded Touch Bar to add a separate Escape key and a separate Touch ID button offline to Touch Bar. The working principle of the Touch ID fingerprint sensor is very similar to the "Touch ID Home" button on an older iPhone. You can use Touch ID instead of a password, and put your finger on the sensor to unlock the Mac. It can also enter passwords for password-protected apps and can be used to purchase Apple Pay Safari.

Touch ID is operated by Apple separated by a T2 chip and Secure Enclave to ensure the security of your fingerprints and personal information.

Thunderstorm 3

All 16-inch computers have four Thunderbolt 3 ports, support USB 3.1 Gen 2 and Thunderbolt 3, and their Thunderbolt transmission speed up to 40Gb / s and USB transmission speed up to 10Gb / s.

Every hole in the MacBook Pro model is the same and can be used for the same function, so the whole port can be used to power the machine. All ports backing the following connections: Power, Thunderbolt, USB, DisplayPort, HDMI, and VGA.

With Thunderbolt 3, the 16-inch MacBook Pro can work simultaneously to display 6K displays or four 4K displays. All external indicators are capable of operating at 60 Hz frequency.

T2 chip

All 16-inch MacBook Pro models include the Apple T2 chip made by Apple to make it more secure and add some features.

The T2 chip is equipped with a Secure Enclave Processor, which protects Touch ID fingerprint data and supports secure startup and encryption functions. It also includes many controllers, including system controllers, image signal processors, audio controllers, and SSD controllers.

It supports advanced tone map creation, advanced display controls, and automatic exposure based on face recognition on FaceTime HD cameras, and uses dedicated AES hardware to instantly encrypt SSD.

The T2 chip also provides "Hey Siri" function support on the

MacBook Pro. With the Hey Siri feature, you can say "Hey Siri" to activate your assistant on your MacBook Pro without pressing the visible Siri button. The T2 chip is different from the A10 on Apple iOS devices and uses a modified version of iOS.

Speaker

The 16-inch MacBook Pro has a very high-end audio system with six speakers. Apple says the six-speaker setup is designed to give artists, podcasters, and video editors the "most advanced audio experience ever made by a laptop."

The speaker system uses Apple's built-in low-powered woofers with two-speaker speakers to minimize unnecessary vibrations that may interfere with the sound. The lead music sounds clearer and more natural, with a deep octave of bass.

Apple said the improved microphone setting could reduce hiss by 40% while improving the signal-to-noise ratio, which Apple says is similar to popular high-tech microphones.

Intel processor

Apple's 16-inch MacBook Pro is the company's largest and most powerful computer, equipped with up to 8-core processors, standalone graphics of AMD Radeon Pro 5000M, up to 64GB of memory, up to 8TB of storage SSD and more The 16-inch display separates it from the 13-inch MacBook Pro and previous 15-inch MacBook Pro models.

The 16-inch MacBook Pro is equipped with Intel's 9th generation 14-nanometer and 14-nanometer Coffee Lake Refresh chips, which are the same chips used in the 15-inch model released in May 2019.

The entry-level 16-inch MacBook Pro uses an Intel 6-core 2.6GHz Core i7 processor with a 4.5GHz Turbo Boost processor. The high-end 16-inch MacBook Pro has Intel's 2.3GHz 8-core 9th-generation Core i9 processor and 4.8GHz Turbo Boost. Both devices can be upgraded to a 2.4GHz 8-core 9th-generation Core i9 processor with Turbo Boost up to 5GHz.

According to Apple, the performance of its 8-core chip is twice as fast as that of a quad-core MacBook Pro, while its performance is 40% higher than that of a 6-core MacBook Pro, making it a chip fast on Mac computer books.

The 16-inch MacBook Pro uses an updated heat purifier, while Apple aims to make the laptop run at higher power for longer.

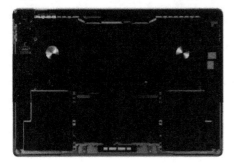

There is a new fan design where the impeller is larger, longer blades, larger blades, and larger ventilation holes, which increases air flow by 28%. The heat sink has risen by 35%, distributing more "more" heat than before, making the 16-inch MacBook Pro more than 12 watts of power during strenuous exercise compared to the previous 15-inch MacBook Pro.

In our test, Apple's heat dissipation enhancement on the 16-inch MacBook Pro increased multi-core performance by 16.5%. The 16-inch MacBook Pro has 989 single points and 6733 multi-core scores, while the previous 15-inch MacBook Pro with the same processor got 972 in one test and 5781 in -multi- basic test. Basic testing.

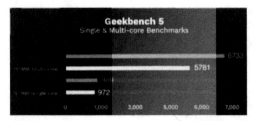

We also used Final Cut Pro and Premier Pro in several performance tests, and our video should be watched to understand how the 16-inch MacBook Pro works when performing "Pro" functions.

Photo card

The 16-inch MacBook Pro model has an Intel built-in UHD Graphics 630 but also equipped with graphics cards for the AMD Radeon Pro 5000M, which are the first GPUs of 7-nanometer mobile discrete GPUs.

The basic 16-inch MacBook Pro has AMD Radeon Pro 5300M with 4GB GDDR6 memory, and the mid-range model has AMD Radeon Pro 5500M with 4GB GDDR6 memory. Both can be upgraded with the AMD Radeon Pro 5500M GPU with 8GB GDDR6 memory, and in June 2020, Apple added a new high-end AMD Radeon Pro 5600M with 8GB HBM2 memory.

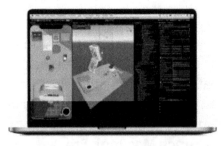

According to Apple, customers who prefer standard GPU configurations see graphics performance 2.1 times higher than previous standard configurations, while customers opting for the higher graphical design option see 80% faster performance than previous advanced configurations.

Apple said that compared to the previous generation 8-core 15-inch MacBook Pro, the 16-inch model with the highest graphics options has the following improvements:

- Video editors using DaVinci Resolve can see 3.4 times faster rendering when doing color editing.
- In games like "Fortress Night", gamers can enjoy a fast gaming experience and get up to 2.6 times performance improvements.
- In combination, developers can get 3.2 times the browsing performance during game development.

When we tested the new 5500M GPU on the final machine, we found great benefits. In the OpenCL test, the 16-inch MacBook Pro got 30 608, while the 15-inch MacBook Pro got 17,904. In the test, the 16-inch MacBook Pro got 29,840, and The 15-inch MacBook Pro gained 29,840. 19065.

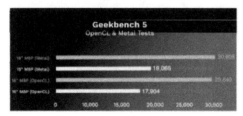

RAM

The 16-inch MacBook Pro supports up to 64GB of 2666MHz DDR4 RAM, faster than the RAM used in previous models. The previous 15-inch MacBook Pro also has up to 32GB of RAM.

SSD

Apple introduced the fastest SSDs in 2016 with consecutive read speeds of up to 3.2GB / s and consecutive write speeds of up to 2.2GB / s, and the same technology has been used on SSD models of the 2019 MacBook Pro.

The 16-inch basic MacBook Pro storage space starts from 512GB but can be upgraded from 4TB to 8TB for the first time.

Camera
Compared to the previous generation of computers, the 16-inch MacBook Pro camera has not yet been upgraded. It continues to use the 720p FaceTime HD camera.

Battery life
Apple's 16-inch MacBook Pro offers "all-day" battery life, wireless network time is up to 11 hours, Apple TV movie playing time is up to 11 hours, and standby time is up to 30 days.

The device has a 99.8 watt-hour lithium polymer battery, which has a higher battery capacity than the 2019 15-inch MacBook Pro model. Apple increased the battery capacity by increasing the battery life of the MacBook Pro. The device comes with a 96W power adapter for USB-C charging.

Wireless communication
Bluetooth 5.0 is built-in in the 2019 16-inch MacBook Pro. It also supports 802.11ac Wi-Fi.

You want answers

MacBook Pro security features
MacBook Pro provides security features that can protect computer content and prevent unauthorized software downloads during the initial process

- Safe storage: The MacBook Pro storage drive is encrypted with a key attached to its hardware to provide advanced security. In the event of a disastrous failure, data recovery may not be likely, so you need to back up your files to an external source. See Apple's support article "About Encrypted Storage on a New Mac". You can set Time Machine or other backup programs to back up your computer regularly. See "Using Time Machine to Back Up Files" in the "MacOS User Guide" and Apple's article support "Using Time Machine to Back Up Your Mac".
- Safe boot and boot utility safe: Safe boot supports automatic unlock. It is designed to ensure that the software installed on the computer was originally powered by Apple. See Apple's support article "About Safe Boot."

If the MacBook Pro fails to start with boots due to unreliable discovery, it will open up from a secure partition and automatically fix the problem if possible. To learn more about "Starting Security Utility" or to learn how to set up some options (for example, boot from an external device), see the Apple Support Article "About Starting a Security Service."

- System integrity (applies to Apple M1 chip only): The Apple M1 chip is designed to ensure that the macOS software version downloaded for the first time is approved by Apple and continues to secretly protect the established macOS authentication while macOS is running. This makes it very difficult for malware or malicious websites to take advantage of your Mac.

- Data protection (Apple M1 chip only): In addition to the automatic drive encryption that uses the Apple M1 chip on the MacBook Pro, third-party application developers can use advanced file encryption to better protect sensitive data without affecting system performance.

Note: In rare cases, such as power outages during the MacOS upgrade process, the MacBook Pro may not respond and may need to restore the firmware to the T2 chip. See Apple support article "Restore or restore Mac firmware to Apple Configurator 2."

Learn more. Please refer to Apple's support article "About Apple T2 Security Chip".

Mac resources, services, and support
You can find more information about the MacBook Pro in system reports, Apple diagnoses, and online resources.

System report. For details on the MacBook Pro, use the program report. Indicates which Hardware and software are installed, serial number and operating system type, how much memory is installed To open "System Report", select the "Apple"> "About this Mac" menu, and click on "System Report".

Apple Diagnosis. You can use Apple Diagnostics to help determine if there is a problem with a part of your computer (such as memory or processor). Apple Diagnostics can help you determine the cause of a potential hardware problem and provide a first step in trying to resolve the problem. If you need further assistance, Apple Diagnostics will also help you contact AppleCare.

Before using Apple Diagnostics, disconnect all external devices, such as hard drives or external displays. Make sure the MacBook Pro is connected to the Internet.

To start Apple Diagnostics on a MacBook Pro using the Apple M1 chip, restart the computer, press and hold the power button for 10 seconds to turn on "Startup Options", then press and hold Command-D to enter Mode mode Diagnostics. To start Apple Diagnostics on some MacBook Pro models, restart the computer and hold the D key for the first time.

When prompted, select your local language. Press Return or click the right arrow button. The basic test of Apple Diagnostics takes a few minutes to complete. If a problem is found, the description of the problem and other instructions will be displayed. If you need to contact AppleCare, please write down all the reference codes before Apple Diagnostics is out.

Online resources. For online service information and support information, go to "Welcome to Apple Support". You can learn about Apple products, browse online brochures, check for software updates, contact other Apple users, and get Apple's services, support, and advice. For more information on MacBook Pro, please visit MacBook Pro Support.

AppleCare support. If you need help, an AppleCare representative can help you install and open the app and resolve the issue. Call your nearest help center (free for the first 90 days). When making a call, please set a purchase date and serial number for the MacBook Pro.

For a complete list of support phone numbers, please visit the Apple website for assistance and service. Phone numbers can change at any time, and country and home values can be used.

Your 90-day free support starts from the date of purchase.

macOS User Guide
The macOS User Guide provides more details on how to use your MacBook Pro.

Get help. Tap the Finder icon in the Dock, then tap the "Help" menu in the menu bar, then select "MacOS Help" to open the macOS User Guide. Or type a question or word in the search field and select a topic from the results list.

Check the title. To find the topic in the macOS User Guide, you can browse or search. To browse, click "Table of Contents" to see a list of topics, and then click a title to read it. Or type what you want in the search field to get the exact answer.

Learn about new features. Click the "Help" menu and select "See what's new in macOS" to learn more about the latest macOS features.

Tip: If you do not remember the location of the menu item in the app, please search for "Help". Place the cursor on the result and the arrow will show you the command.

Save space on MacBook Pro

With Backup Setup, you can automatically free up space on

your MacBook Pro by providing files on demand. Your original files will be stored on iCloud and IMAP email or Exchange server, so you can download them at any time. Some tools can identify and delete large files.

Configure storage. To view storage recommendations, go to Apple menu> About this Mac, click Storage, and then click Manage. Depending on how you set up your Mac, you'll see various suggestions. If you do not have enough storage space on your Mac, you will see a warning with a link in the store window.

Set options to:

- Save to iCloud: Save all files, photos, and messages to iCloud and save space on your Mac.
  - Desktop and Documents: Save all files in the "Desktop and Documents" folder on Cloud Drive. When storage space is required, Cloud Drive will store newly opened files on Mac and provide older files as needed.
  - Photos: Save photos and videos to iCloud photos. When storage space is required, iCloud photos will use advanced types of photos and videos on Mac and provide real-time on-demand.
  - Email: Save all emails and attachments to iCloud. When storage space is required, iCloud will store the latest attachments to the Mac and provide the oldest files as needed.
- Even if your files are stored in the cloud, you can still access them where you left them on your MacBook Pro.

Access your iCloud content on Mac.

- Customize storage: Save space on your Mac by storing movie and TV programs in the Apple TV program. You can choose to automatically uninstall it from MacBook Pro after viewing MacBook Pro. You can download them all over at any time.
- Automatically remove garbage: Automatically delete items that have been in the trash for more than 30 days.
- Reduce confusion: easily identify large files and delete unwanted files. To browse large files, click the sidebar - books, documents, iCloud drive, email, messages, create music, photos, dump paper, etc.

To help you save space, MacOS will also do the following:

- Prevent yourself from downloading the same file from Safari twice
- Remember to uninstall the software when you have finished installing the new applications
- Clear logs and storage that can be safely removed when storage space is limited

Frequently asked questions about Mac

How can I get support for MacBook Pro? Go to MacBook Pro support.

I'm new to Mac. Are there any tips for PC users? Yes, that's right! See Apple Support Tips for Mac Tips for Windows Switchers. Check out a quick visit to Mac Basics. You may be interested in keyboard shortcuts on Mac.

How to take a screenshot on a Mac? Press Command-Shift-3 to take a full screenshot. Press Command-Shift-4 to take a screenshot of the selected location on the screen. To learn more, see Taking a screenshot on a Mac.

What is my serial number? Select the "Apple" menu> "About this Mac". The serial number is the last item on the list. You can also find the serial number at the bottom of the MacBook Pro.

Ask Siri. Say a bit like: "What is the serial number of my super-computer?"

How do I know which MacBook Pro model I have? See the Apple support article "Find your MacBook Pro model." You can also select the Apple menu> About this device to view model details.

How to get MacBook Pro documents? For the Essentials guide, select the Apple menu> "About this Mac", click the "Support" tab, and then click on "User Manual." On the "Support" tab, you can also click "MacOS Help" to open the app's user guide. For older Mac models, please refer to product browsing manuals.

How can I get help with the app? When using the app, click the "Help" menu in the menu bar at the top of the screen.

What is the security information for the MacBook Pro? Please see the important Mac security details.

How can you get technical specifications? Go to MacBook Pro technical specifications, or select Apple> About Mac, then click the Up button.

Ask Siri. Ask Siri for details about the Mac. Say this:

- "How fast is my Mac?"
- "How much money does my Mac have?"
- "How much free space is there on my Mac?"
- "How much space do I leave in iCloud storage?"

How can you check if there is a problem with the disk? Use Disk Utility. Please refer to the "Disk Utility User Guide" in Disk Utility on Mac to configure storage devices.

What should I do before selling or trading on a Mac? Back up data, and restore Mac to factory settings. Before you sell, offer, or trade your Mac, see what you do.

How do you reinstall macOS? Use macOS to restore. (The MacOS Pro recovery process with the Apple M1 chip is different from other MacBook Pro models.) Please see how to reinstall macOS in macOS recovery.

Note: Starting with macOS Big Sur, Time Machine backups do not include program files. See Back up and Restore the Mac.

Take a screenshot on a Mac

Browse through the "Screenshot" menu to find all the controls needed to take screenshots and screen videos. You can also take a voice during screen recording. Customized workflow allows you to take photos and videos on screen, and easily share, edit or save them.

Access screen control. Press Command-Shift-5. You can capture the entire screen, the selected window, or part of the window. You can record the entire screen or selected parts of the screen.

Use the icons at the bottom of the screen to capture the selection, the "screen selection option" icon, the recording screen, the "record screen" icon, and more. Click on options to change your storage location, set the timer before shooting, set the microphone and audio options, or display directions. Click Take or Record to take a screenshot or video.

After taking a screenshot or video, an icon will appear in the corner of the screen. Drag the icon to the document or folder, swipe right to save it quickly, or click edit or share.

Note: You can also open the "Screenshot" app from the "Other" folder in the launchpad, or go to the "Applications"> "Applications" folder in Finder.

Tag your screenshot. Click on the screenshot icon to use the marking tool and define it. You can also click the "Share" icon to send a marked screen to colleagues or friends directly from the screen itself. See marking files on Mac in macOS user directory

Keyboard shortcuts for Mac

You can press a key combination to perform tasks that you would normally use a trackpad, mouse, or another device to perform on your MacBook Pro. The following is a list of the most commonly used keyboard shortcuts.

Commandment-X

Cut out the nominated item and copy it to the clipboard.

Commandment-C

Copy the selected item to the paste board.

Commandment-V

Paste the clipboard contents into the current document or application.

Command-Z

Undo the last command. Press Command-Shift-Z to reset.

Commandment-A

Select all items.

Command-F

Open the Discover window, or search for items in this document.

Command-G

Find the next match for the item you want. Press Command-

Shift-G to get the latest experience.

Command-H

Hide previous app window. Press Command-Option-H to view previous applications, but hide all other applications

Command-M

Minimize the front Dock window. Press Command-Option-M to minimize all windows of the previous application.

Command-N

Open a new document or window.

Command-O

Open the selected item, or open a dialog box to select a file to open.

Command-P

Print the current document.

Command-S

Keep the current document.

Command-W

Close the front window. Press Command-Option-W to close all application windows.

Command-Q

Exit the current app.

Command-Option-Esc

Select an application to force quit.

Command-Tab

Switch to the next application used between open applications.

Command-Shift-5

Turn on screenshot usage. You can also use the following shortcuts to take screenshots:

Press Command-Shift-3 to take a full screenshot.

Press Command-Shift-4 to take a screenshot of the selected location on the screen.

Press Command-Shift-6 to capture the touch bar.

If you are switching from PC to Mac, please see the Apple support Mac Tips article for Windows Switcher for a list of Mac keyboard shortcuts and differences between Mac and Windows keyboards, and what's the name on Mac? For more keyboard shortcuts, check out Apple Keyboard shortcuts.

Apps

How to set up FaceTime on a Mac

Here's how to get started with FaceTime, a Mac built-in video and audio streaming app.

While "message" is a great way to send short messages to friends, sometimes you want to talk to people. That's where FaceTime comes in. When your communication requires a personal style, FaceTime can enable you to make video and audio calls with people.

Follow this guide to learn how to use FaceTime for Mac.

- How to set up FaceTime on a Mac
- How to make a call on FaceTime
- How to enter an email address on FaceTime
- How to choose a number or email address to call on FaceTime
- How to set FaceTime ringtones
- How to set your location on FaceTime

How to set up FaceTime on a Mac

Getting started with FaceTime is very easy, you only need an Apple ID.

1. Open FaceTime on your Mac.
2. Enter your Apple ID email address and password, then click "Sing". If you have enabled 2-step verification or

two-factor verification in your Apple ID, please enter your verification code.

How to make a call on FaceTime

Put your phone in your pocket or desk, and use FaceTime to make the next call.

1. Open FaceTime on your Mac.
2. If you want to make a new call, click the search bar.

3. Enter the name, phone number, or email address you want to contact.
4. Click Audio or Video to choose how to contact that person.

5. Click on FaceTime Audio or contact phone number (if Audio is selected).

How to enter an email address on FaceTime

If you have multiple email addresses or aliases, you can set up your account so you can access them all on FaceTime. But you have not set it in the FaceTime app. Instead, you need to go to "System Preferences."

1. Open "System Favorites" from the Dock folder or "Applications".
2. Click Apple ID.

3. Click name, phone, email.
4. Click the + button under the "Accessible" section.

5. Enter the email address you need to use.
6. Click Next.

7. When prompted, enter the verification code sent to that email address. Your code will be automatically verified.

You should now be able to contact you with the email address you entered.

How to choose a number or email address to call on FaceTime

Choose a phone number or email address that you will recognize when calling people using FaceTime.

1. When you open FaceTime, click FaceTime in the menu bar.
2. Click Favorites.

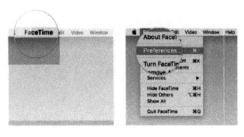

3. Click the drop-down menu next to starting a new call.
4. Select the email address or phone number you want to use to start a
new call.

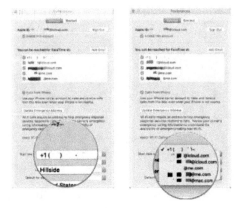

How to set FaceTime ringtones

Customize your FaceTime experience with new ringtones.

1. When you open FaceTime, click FaceTime in the menu bar.
2. Click Favorites.

3. Click the drop-down menu next to the ringtone.
4. Choose the ringtone you like.

How to set your location on FaceTime

1. When you open FaceTime, click FaceTime in the menu bar.
2. Click Favorites.

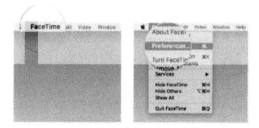

3. Click the drop-down menu near the location.
4. Choose a location that you like.

How to get started with Mac App Store

How to use the App Store on Mac?

The App Store on Mac is a hole in the expanded library. Gone are the days of buying computer programs at electronics stores. You can download any content you want from the App Store. Some things are free. Some expenses you have to pay. You only need an Apple ID and you can leave.

Here's how to get started on a Mac App Store!

- How to log in with your Apple ID
- How to sight and correct your Apple ID account
- How to download apps or games
- How to set up automatic download of apps or games on another Mac
- How to get apps or games after installation
- How to view and reload apps and games you previously purchased
- How to check for updates in Mac App Store apps
- How to enable automatic updates

How to log in with your Apple ID

Before you can download any app, you need to sign in with your Apple ID.

1. Launch the App Store from Dock or Finder below "Requests".
2. Click Login in the lower-left corner
3. Enter your Apple ID and password.

4. Click to log in or press the keyboard input key.

How to assess and edit your Apple ID account

Before you download the app, you need to make sure payment and country/region details are correct, so you can ignore these things when you are excited to download the app.

1. Launch the App Store from Dock or Finder.
2. tap your name on the left side of the display screen. It should be in the corner.

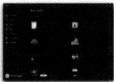

3. Click View Details in the top right corner. Here, you can edit your credit card details, billing address, country/region, and nickname. If you are planning a nickname, the nickname will be displayed in this way in the Game Center.
4. Type the required information in the field for the item you want to edit.

If you are satisfied with the conversion, please click the blue "Finish" button!

How to download apps or games

Whether the purpose is to increase productivity or waste time, the App Store can provide you with apps. You just need to download it. Here's how to do it:

1. Launch the App Store from Dock or Finder.
2. Search for the app you need to download. You can outlook installed apps or search by category, title, etc.
3. If it is a paid program, click on the price; If it is a free application, click Get.
4. If it is a paid app, click "Buy app"; if free, click "Apply"
5. Enter your Apple ID password.
6. Click Buy. (Even if the program is free, it will show "Purchased").

How to set up automatic download of apps or games on another Mac

When you download apps and games on different Macs, you can enable the default download feature so that all the apps are available on all Macs!

1. Launch the App Store from Dock or Finder.
2. Click the App Store in the menu bar at the top left of the screen.
3. Click Favorites.
4. Click the checkbox next to automatically downloading apps purchased from other Macs.

How to get apps or games after installation

After downloading the app, you want to find and use it. Here's how to do it right!

1. Open a recovery window.
2. Click "Applications" in the left-hand folder.
3. Click the settings button at the top of the window. Looks like gears.
4. Click Edit.
5. Click Add Date. This will move your recently downloaded apps to the top of the list.

How to view and reload apps and games you previously purchased

If you have already paid for the application, you do not need to pay again. So, if it is lost, you can download it again without going too far!

1. Launch the App Store from Dock or Finder.
2. Click your name in the lower-left corner of the window.
3. Click Download next to the app or game you want to download again.

How to check for updates in Mac App Store apps

It's a good idea to make sure your entire download system has the latest version. The test method is as follows:

1. Launch the App Store from Dock or Finder.
2. Click Update in the left column of the window.
3. Click Update next to each app you want to update or click Update all.
4. When prompted, enter your Apple ID password.

How to enable automatic updates

If you have too many apps, it can be painful to keep them all and regularly check for updates. You can set automatic updates to do this to you!

1. Launch the App Store from Dock or Finder.
2. Click the App Store in the menu bar at the top left of the screen.
3. Click Favorites.
4. Click the check box next to automatically check for updates.
5. Click the checkbox next to the setting for each update you want to enable:
   ○ Download the latest updates available in the background

- Install app updates
- Install macOS updates
- Install system data files and security updates

map

Use maps or satellite imagery to get directions and view places. Get the best in town tips from Apple's carefully selected guide. Force push into place to place a pushpin on it.

Explore new places with your guide. To help you find the best places to eat, shop, and explore around the world, the map offers selected guidelines provided by trusted products and partners. You can keep these guidelines and update them when you add new locations.

Create your guide. You can create your guide to your favorite places and share them with friends and family. To create a guide, hover over the "My Guide" in the sidebar, click the "Add" icon on the right, then hold down the Ctrl key and click on the new guide to see the options menu.

3D test. Click the "Looking Around Binoculars" icon to browse the selected city in 3D and cross the streets smoothly in a connected way.

View internal maps of major locations. Find your way out near certain airports and major shopping malls. Just zoom in to see restaurants near your door, find toilets, arrange a meeting place with friends at the mall, and more.

Ask Siri. Say something like this: "Get coffee near me."

Take public transportation to get there. The map provides details of the public transportation of a particular city. Click the destination bar in the sidebar, and then click the navigation icon to get the suggested route and estimated travel time.

Scheduling an electric car ride becomes easier. Install your electric car on your iPhone, and Google Maps will show you the location of the charging station on the route and consider the charging time when the ETA counts.

Plan your bike route. The map gives you the information you need to plan your bike rides, such as altitude, traffic conditions, and whether there are small slopes. After planning your trip, you can send it to your iPhone.

Get real-time ETA updates. When friends and family members share their estimated time of arrival with you, a map can show you where they are on the route.

Warning: For important information about roaming and to avoid potential interference, please refer to your Mac's safety features.

Tip: To view traffic, click the "View" menu in the menu bar, then select "Show Traffic".

How to set up and use "Find My" on Mac

Find the most important family members and devices on your Mac.

The "I Found" app is available on a variety of devices, including iPhone, iPad, and Mac. The app includes the old "Find My iPhone" and "Find My Friends" apps. Here's how to use the Find My app on macOS Big Sur.

Is there a new Mac on the market? Check out our best iMacs and best MacBook posts of the year.

How to use my stuff on Mac

macOS will automatically install Find Me. Available on Mac Dock and the "Applications" folder. Use the app to track your friends on the device.

Follow your friends with "Find My Friends" on Mac

On the "People" screen, you'll see a list of people who can access it.

1. Open "Find my app" on your Mac.
2. Click the People tab.
3. Select the person you want to follow to the left of the screen. You can assess a person on three maps: default, hybrid, and satellite.
4. Click-then + to change the map size.

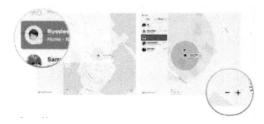

5. Select a location icon to find your current location on the map.

6. Click Share My Location to send your current location to new friends.
7. In the "To" box, type the name of the person you want to share your location with.
8. If someone is not in your "Contacts" program, please add them to the popup menu.
9. After adding a new person, select Send.

Use " Found my" on Mac to track devices

Devices under the "I Found" app are available on devices related to your Apple ID and your family.

1. Open "Find my app" on your Mac.
2. Click the Device tab.
3. Select the device you want to track on the left side

of the screen. You can view devices on three standard maps: default, hybrid, and satellite.

4. Click-then + to change the map size.
5. Select a location icon to find your current location on the map.

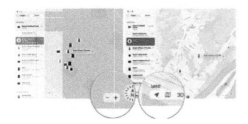

How to Get Started with Safari on Mac

Need help getting started on Safari? Here's how to do it right!

Safari is Apple's web browser - your website. You can visit the website, add bookmarks to your favorite pages, etc. This is the information you need to start using Safari on Mac on macOS Big Sur.

How to find a website

The main purpose of Safari is to provide you with an Internet site, that is, millions of websites. If you know the web address or "URL" of the website you want to visit, you can enter it manually.

1. Launch Safari from Dock or Finder.
2. tap the address bar at the up of the window.
3. Enter the address of the website you want to visit, for example,
4. Press Enter on the keyboard.

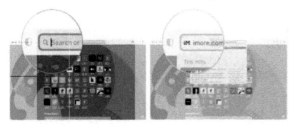

How to search using the address bar

You can type a website with the URL in the address bar, for example, www.imore.com. But this is not just a URL; you can also use it to search Google!

1. Launch Safari from Dock or Finder.
2. tap the address bar at the up of the window.
3. Enter a search query, such as "funny cat videos".
4. Press Enter on the keyboard.

Safari will redirect you to Google, where you will see a list of search results.

How to book a website

If you like reading online, or want immediate access to your favorite website, you can add it as a bookmark so you can come back with one click later!

1. Launch Safari on Mac from Dock or Finder.
2. Go to the web page you want to tag.
3. Press Command-D on the keyboard.
4. Enter a bookmark title, or leave it as needed. You can also enter a description as needed.
5. Press Enter or press Enter on the keyboard.

6. Select View in the menu bar at the top left of the screen.
7. Select to show the favorites bar.

Now, bookmarked pages you have added to "Favorites" will be displayed below the address bar so you can visit each page with a single click. Additionally, whenever you click on the address bar, your favorites will be displayed as suggested sites.

How to view all bookmarks

If you do not want to set preferences under the address bar, or you want to keep your bookmarks in a separate folder, you can view all your bookmarks at once.

1. Launch Safari from Dock or Finder.
2. Click the sidebar button next to the address bar.
3. Click the Bookmarks tab (if not available). It looks like a book.

How to delete bookmarks

If you no longer need the page because you no longer need the page or the page no longer exists, you can delete it from your bookmarks.

1. Launch Safari on Mac from Dock or Finder.
2. Select the bookmarks in the menu bar at the top left of the screen.
3. Click Edit Bookmark.
4. Select the bottom left arrow of "Favorites."

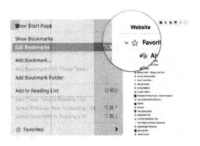

5. Right-click or Control-click the bookmark you want to delete.
6. Click Delete.

How to add a web page to a reading list

After adding a page to the reading list, you can save the site and read it later. The best part is that you can even view the reading list offline.

1. Launch Safari from Dock or Finder.
2. Go to the website you want to add to your reading list.
3. Press the shift-D key on the keyboard or select "Book-marks" from the menu bar, then select "Add to reading list".

That's all you need to do is add a web page to your reading list! You will see a small icon reach the sidebar or a side button.

How you look at your reading list

If you want to save pages in your reading list, you will want to view them again! Here's how to do it right!

1. Launch Safari on Mac from Dock or Finder.
2. Select the display button next to the address bar.
3. Select a reading list tab. It looks like mirrors.
4. Click the item you want to view.

How to remove items from the reading list

After you have finished reading the list item, you can delete it so that you do not have to browse the web pages you have already browsed.

1. Launch Safari from Dock or Finder.
2. Click the sidebar button next to the address bar.
3. Select a reading list tab. It looks like mirrors.
4. Right-click or control the item you want to delete.
5. Click Delete item.

How to enable private browsing

Private browsing allows you to browse the Internet without having to store websites you've been to, search history, or auto-fill details. This is an excellent choice when buying or buying Christmas presents on a shared computer.

1. Launch Safari on Mac from Dock or Finder.
2. Click File in the menu bar at the top left of the screen.
3. Click New Dedicated Window. You can press the shift-N button on the keyboard.

Now, any websites you visit or auto-fill details will not be saved, so no one can track your whereabouts based on historical records.

How to View a Website Privacy Report

Starting with macOS Big Sur, you can now view security reports on all websites you visit. to date:

1. Launch Safari from Dock or Finder.
2. Go to the website you want to visit.
3. Click the Privacy Report button to the left of the address bar.
4. Select the details icon to view the full report.

5. View this report, which contains a list of trackers iS Safari that prevents you from running on the website.
6. Click the red circle in the upper left corner to exit the report.

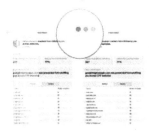

How to add extensions to Safari

Browser extensions plug-ins add new features to Safari. They can do things like block ads, integrate with apps, and so on. There are many free extensions to help you improve your work efficiency, keep up to date with the latest news, provide security, entertainment, and other features!

Note: Although extensions are free, applications or services that offer extensions may not be free.

1. Launch Safari from Dock or Finder.
2. In the menu bar at the top left of the screen, click Safari.
3. Click on Safari extension.

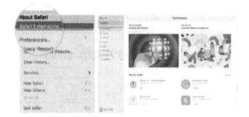

You will be redirected to the Safari extension page of the Mac App Store, where you can download and install extensions, such as downloading and installing any other apps in the Mac App Store. After the installation is complete, open the app to install it in the Safari toolbar.

How to edit the label

Like adding a website to your "Favorites", you can pin down the label to visit the websites you visit the most with one click.

1. Launch Safari from Dock or Finder.
2. Click View in the menu bar at the top left of the screen.
3. Click to display a tab line.
4. Go to the website you want to install.

5. Click and hold the tab, then drag it to the left. The tab will now appear as a small site icon or the first character of the site title on the left side of the tab bar.
6. To remove a fixed label, just drag it to the right.

How to set up a homepage

By default, Safari will open access to apple.com when it first launches. If you want to create another website on the homepage, you can.

1. Launch Safari from Dock or Finder.
2. In the menu bar at the top left of the screen, click Safari.
3. Select "Preferences" and confirm that the "General" tab.
4. Put the website next to the homepage. Or, if you want your current page to be a home page, you can click on "Set as current page".

5. Click the drop-down menu next to Open a new win-

dow.

6. If you want to open a new window on the Home page, click "Home".
7. Click the drop-down menu next to opening a new tab.
8. If you want to open a new tab page, click "Home".

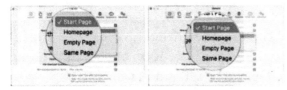

How to customize the home page

From MacOS Big Sur, you can set up the home page. You can set a background image and select a new category to be displayed on the home page including "Favorites", "Privacy Suggestions", "Reading List", "iCloud Tags" and "Privacy Reports".

1. Launch Safari from Dock or Finder. By default, unless you make changes using the drop-down menu above, the home page will be automatically launched. On this page, you'll find the following categories: Favorites, Frequent Visits, Privacy Report, Siri Suggestions, Readlists, and Cloud Tab.
2. Click the settings icon in the lower right corner of the home page to make changes.
3. Uncheck the parts you don't want to see.
4. Select the background to change or add your own.

How to share a website

If you come across a web page that you want your friends or family members to see, you can share it in many ways.

1. Launch Safari from Dock or Finder.
2. Go to the website you want to share.
3. Click the form sharing button at the top right of the Safari window.
4. Choose a way to share. You can share emails, notes, reminders, messages, AirDrop, and apps of foreign companies.

How to use a student view

Reader View allows you to use a more advanced script to drag web pages, read words and view images without having to write many beautiful pictures or move the page. Not all web pages support Reader View, but many do. This is how it works.

1. Navigate to the web page.
2. Click the Viewer View button. This is the line on the left side of the address bar.

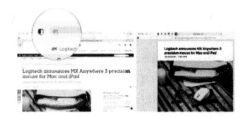

How to change background color in Reader View

1. Navigate to the web page.
2. Click the Viewer View button. This is the line on the left side of the address bar.
3. Click the Reader Options button. These two Asss are

on the right side of the address bar.

4. Click on the back bar if you want to use it.

How to change the font in Reader View.

1. Navigate to the web page.
2. Click the Viewer View button. This is the line on the left side of the address bar.
3. Click the Reader Options button. These two Asss are on the right side of the address bar.
4. Click the font you want to use.

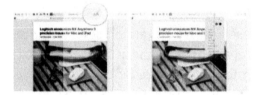

How to change the font size in Reader View.

1. Navigate to the web page.
2. Click the Viewer View button. This is the line on the left side of the address bar.
3. Click the Reader Options button. These two Asss are on the right side of the address bar.
4. Click A to make the text bigger or smaller. A smaller "A" will reduce text size, and a larger "A" will increase the text size.

How to set up and start using photos on Mac

You can save, edit, share, edit, and much more in the Mac "Photos" app. Here's how to get started!

Apple's Mac version of Photos lays a solid foundation for iPhoto and iOS photos and can provide users like you a quick and portable way to manage, edit and share all photos (without pressure).

Plus, with a tag editor, you can use your memory and do great things!

Whether this is your first time using a photo management app, upgrading from iPhoto, or exploring the open or Lightroom streets, this is what you need to know about photos on macOS!

Getting started with photos on Mac

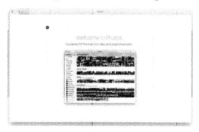

When you open a photo for the first time, it will show you a full view of what the app will look like after uploading all the photos, videos, and memories. You will get the results you want quickly.

Another way to use the "Photos" app is the ability to create physical memories, such as calendars, collages, cups, etc., but they are only available in the United States, Canada, Japan, and other European and Asia-Pacific countries.

The introduction will show you how to organize and split photos.

- Should you use the iCloud Photo Library?

From here, your route will vary, depending on whether you are new to image management or a previous iPhoto, Aperture, or Lightroom user.

If you are new to handling photos on Mac

Do you have random image folders to watch from your desktop? Ever used other Mac photo apps like Apple or Aperture? Using "Photos", you can easily find content on your desktop and iPhone, and add this content to "Photos" on your Mac and cloud.

After completing the initial setup process, you can start by uploading photos and videos or taking a tour. If you are unfamiliar with photos, then a tour is the best choice!

After the trip, you can continue ...

- Connect the camera or memory card
- Drag the image directly to "Photos"
- Select the import from the file menu
- Open the Cloud Photo Library preferences

... That way, you can start uploading photos!

If you want to upgrade from iPhoto or Aperture

Starting with macOS Catalina, The Hole no longer works. You can still use "Photos" to select your open library, as shown below, but this may only show original images and not the edits you made. Apple will issue an update to macOS Catalina to resolve this issue. Until then, you should save the Aperture library and hope to move it to "Photos" again.

Apple announced in 2014 that it would no longer be able to continue developing iPhoto or Aperture, the latter being an old system for storing and editing Macs. Instead, the company introduced Photos. If you have resisted this change, but have finally decided to switch to "Photos" on your Mac, it won't be as painful as you think.

If there is only one iPhoto library on your Mac, the library should be upgraded automatically after opening the "Photos" program. If you need to use iPhoto for any reason, the old iPhoto library will remain, but changes made to these old photos will not be automatically synced to the new library.

If you have multiple libraries on your computer, Pictures will ask you to choose which library to import. Unfortunately, you cannot combine multiple libraries in a single image library - you must select the one you want to use. If you need to do this, you can use Aperture to compile the library first, and then import the integrated library to Pictures. However, except for manual migration, there is no better way to import existing image libraries.

Note for users wishing to switch to Lightroom

If you have switched to Lightroom in the past, but now want to move in "Photos", the best option is to upload Lightroom folders and files directly to "Photos". Just be careful where they are stored on the hard drive and import them.

➢ How to sync Lightroom export with photos on Mac

How to import photos and folders into photos

After setting the photos, the next step is to import the photos. This is the information you need when importing old photos and libraries in the Mac Photo version.

1. Open "Photos" from the Dock folder or "Applications".
2. Click the file menu.

3. Select import (or type command-Shift-I).
4. Find and select the image you want to import.

5. Click View to download.

6. Verify your photos by clicking to import all new photos in the top right corner.

The file will now be added to your photo library.

In Finder, you can also just drag and drop the image you want to insert into the "Photo" icon. Photos will bring them in.

But keep in mind that the automatic operation of the images should not include the first import image. Maintains a link to them, so you can sort or categorize them using "images", but keep them in their place.

This is a double-edged sword: it reduces the size of the image library, but if your goal is to clear folders and disks that contain too many images, it can confuse you. To put everything in the photo library, make sure you change the image preferences to copy imported files to the photo library. If you plan to share these imported images on other devices, there is another important reason: just download the copied items to the library in the iCloud library.

How to copy imported files into your photo library

1. Open "Photos" and click "Photos".
2. Click Favorites ...

3. See the Copy item to the image library.

Doing so means that only items copied from the library will be uploaded to Cloud Photos.

How to import iPhoto library to macOS images

If you only have one iPhoto library

If you want to upgrade from iPhoto to Mac version photos, and there is a single iPhoto library on your Mac, the development process is simple: after opening the app for the first time, the photos will automatically import all iPhoto photos to the app.

If you need to use iPhoto for any reason, the old iPhoto library will remain, but changes made to these old photos will not be automatically synced to the new library. If you do not need your old iPhoto library, you can dump it - your photos can now be safely stored in photos (and, if you have iCloud Photo Library on, you can be on iCloud)

If you use multiple libraries

Mac version of images is only compatible with one main library on each Mac: this means you cannot combine multiple old iPhoto or Aperture libraries into a single library.

Therefore, if you have multiple libraries on your computer, Images will ask you to select a library to import when you first launch the program. After selecting the gallery you want to use, "Photos" will edit and import these photos.

1. While clicking an image, hold the Option key on the keyboard until a popup menu appears.

2. Click the library you want to open in the "Select Library" window that appears.

3. Click the Select Library button.

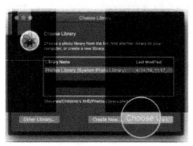

You can still upgrade some old libraries into a separate photo library; you only need to import each one individually by clicking on the images icon when launching the app.

These other photo libraries have the same functionality, except for one: only one library can be synced with the Cloud Photo Library at a time. All of you will be localized (or externally, if you install it on your hard drive) from the iCloud sync service.

How to Import Open Library on Mac version photos

Starting with macOS Catalina, The Hole no longer works. You can still use "Photos" to select your open library, as shown below, but this may only show original images and not the edits you made. Apple will issue an update to macOS Catalina to resolve this issue. Until then, you should save the Aperture library and hope to move it to "Photos" again.

If you want to use the existing open library as your primary library, you only need to select it as part of the initial settings for the Mac version of "Photos".

If you would like to import an opening library as one of the picture libraries, please follow the steps below.

1. Find your open library in Finder, then click on Control or right-click it. The default location is in the "Photos" folder.
2. Move the mouse over the open path.

3. Click the image shown in the menu.

The image will now start and will be uploaded to the library. When you're done, all the pictures in the opening library will be there, and you'll be able to find stacks, items, and events in the sidebar on the left.

How to call EXIF, location, and other metadata information in Mac version images

1. Launch photos on Ma
2. Select the photo or video you want

3. Click on the window.

4. Click Info (or click Command + I).

The info window will display all the data you need, and you can edit the title, description, keywords, faces, and other data in it instantly.

How to add captions, captions, and keywords to photos or videos in Mac version photos

1. Launch Photos on Mac
2. Select the photo or video you want

3. Press Command + I to bring the details of the photos.
4. Click Add Title at the top and enter your title.

5. Click Enter description and enter specific details about the image or video.
6. Click "Enter keyword" and enter other words that may help you find photos or videos in the future, such as "Family", "Bob's 2014 Birthday", "Apple Watch Event", no matter which method you choose.

How to manage keywords with Mac version images

If you are a more powerful keyword user, Photos for Mac will provide you with the most powerful keyword tools.

1. Launch Photos on Mac
2. Press Command + K to bring up the key box.

3. Click on a keyword to apply to the currently selected photo or video. (Or just type in its shortcut.)
4. Click the keyword again to remove it from the currently selected photo or video. (Or enter its shortcut again.)

5. Click "Edit Keyword" to change the current keyword.
6. Click + to enter new keywords and shortcuts, - delete existing keywords and shortcuts, or click Rename to make changes.

How to search for photos and videos in Mac Photos

1. Launch photos on Mac.
2. Click the search bar in the top right corner.

3. Enter the name you want to search for. You can enter more names, such as "Cupertino Lory Apple March 25, 2019"

4. Select the photo or video you want from the "Photo Filler" list.

How to search for an exact category in the "Photos" app

The `` Photos' app has a built-in AI function that can scan your photos and categorize them. This is very difficult (I have a lot of phone pictures, but typing "phone" does not produce results), but if you are looking for pictures of dogs, cats, sunsets, or other images that can go into general categories, this type of search can help you!

1. Launch the "Photos" app on the dock.
2. Click the search bar in the top right corner.

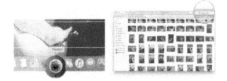

3. Enter the category you want to search for; for example, "coffee".

4. Click the option you want to select. All photos and videos related to the keyword will be displayed.

How to use Smart Album as "Advanced Search" in Mac version of "Photos"

The smart folder system in the Mac version of images "is very smart and offers many options. If you need more complex features than standard search, especially if you think you may not use them often, smart folders can be a good choice.

   ○ How to use smart folders in photos on Mac

How to set it up and start using the home app on Mac

Want to use Mac to control HomeKit-enabled housing? Here's how to do it right!

These days, it's hard not to have smart technology at home.

Smart home technology is ubiquitous, and most of us have some form in our homes. Whether it's a bright light bulb, a door lock, or a camera, almost everything in our home these days has connectivity options. Many of these products also use Apple's HomeKit, so you can control the best HomeKit accessories using your iOS or Mac device using the Siri or Home app. This is a way to use the home app on Mac.

How to set up and start using the Home-based app on Mac:

- How to set up the home app
- Getting started with the home app

How to use the home app on Mac

Unfortunately, you cannot directly set up the Home app on your Mac. Instead, you need to set up an iOS device first.

1. Make sure your HomeKit accessory is turned on and close to your iOS device. You also need to double-check if you need other devices to use iOS (for example, Philips Hue Bridge for Philips Hue bulbs).
2. On your iOS device, launch the Home app.
3. Click the merge icon.

4. Use the device camera to follow the instructions to scan the HomeKit setup code to find accessories.
   ◦ The HomeKit setup code is usually found in the manual that comes with the device itself or the accessory. If you only want to manually enter the verification code, you can also select "I don't have a verification

code" or "I can't scan".

- Some accessories support NFC pairing, and you can make pairing by placing your iPhone next to the Hom-eKit code.

5. Click Add on the homepage.
6. Provide accessories in the room and click Continue.

7. Enter an accessory name and click Continue. If neces-sary, select suggested automation and click Continue.
8. Depending on the accessory, you may see other options during the setup process, such as setting camera notifi-cations and recording options.
9. Click Finish.

To make your HomeKit accessories appear in the Home app on your Mac, you need to sign in with the same Apple ID on both de-vices, and enable the iCloud key and two-way authentication, and it should be set to your iCloud. Both iOS and Mac should be updated with the latest software.

You can't directly add new accessories to the Mac version of the Home app, which is a little disappointing, but you still get some features that Home can offer.

Start using Home in macOS

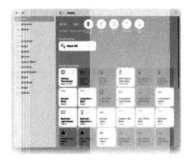

Managing HomeKit accessories for Mac works the same way as for iOS and iPadOS, using taps and right clicks instead of taps and long presses. The macOS Home app also includes a side-by-side navigation view on the iPad, allowing you to easily jump to a specific room without having to browse each room individually.

To turn on / off or view live HomeKit camera feeds, just click on it. A gray icon indicates that the device is currently switched off, and a white icon indicates that the phone is on. Right-click on the device and you'll find two options: "Display controls" or "View Camera and Settings". By using the "Settings" menu, you can perform tasks such as renaming the device, which is very useful when moving items in the house.

Settings will allow you to view the device name and room. From here, you can add the device to the favorites list, add it to status update (include or exclude status updates) (default, included), group attachments, adjust HomeKit security camera options, and view detailed details about device manufacturer, model, the firmware of serial.

When you click on "Display Controls", you will be able to access tasks such as dimming the lights and adjusting the temperature, depending on the device used. For those who use compatible bulbs, "display controls" will also give you the option to change the color of the light and enable flexible lighting.

HomeKit notifications are also available on macOS, and banners appear in the upper right corner of the screen and the control area. As with iOS, you can set notifications to let you open a door or window, or notify you when one of the HomeKit cameras detects motion with icons.

Automation for all

Although MacOS Home seems a bit dull and cannot add accessories, it is still a useful tool with easy controls and notification functions. Using the app home screen on your Mac means you don't have to have an iPhone or tablet on your desk, you can even control lighting or call a real-time HomeKit camera view.

Or, if you want to lower the thermostat of the HomeKit thermostat a bit, and the iOS device is not near you, but you are close to the computer, just do it from there. It's never been easy right now, especially if you're lazy. If you are not satisfied with smart home technology, perhaps the ability to manage a home with a computer will change this situation.

How to set up and start using Mac Mail

How to configure mail settings on Mac? Here's how to do it right!

The Mac's Mail app allows you to use any email account you have without having to visit the service website often. You can sync your Gmail account, Outlook account, carrier account, school account, work account ... well, you'll know.

All necessity is to set it up. This is the way to MacOS Big Sur!

Mail Settings: how to set up an email account

The first step to using the Mail app on your Mac is to set up your email account to start receiving emails in the Mail app.

1. Launch Email from Dock or Finder.
2. Depending on the type of email account you have, click on the email provider. If the domain of the email address you are using is not the one provided (for example, the school or work email address that is not available to any major provider), click "Other Mail Account"
3. Click Continue.
4. Enter your email address and password.

5. Click the tag next to each application you want to use with this account.
6. Click Finish.

If you have multiple email accounts, you can repeat this process to view them all in the Mail app.

Mail Settings: how to set the frequency for viewing new mail

Since the mail system must receive email from any used service, you can set how often to check for new email.

1. Launch Email from Dock or Finder.
2. tap "Mail" in the list of options bar at the top left of the screen.
3. Click Favorites.
4. If you have not already done so, click the "General" tab.
5. Click the drop-down menu next to Check new mail.
6. Click frequency. You can have it checked every minute or every hour. You can also choose to check by hand only.

Mail settings: how to select the post notification sound

You can choose which sound will remind you of the new emails.

1. Launch Email from Dock or Finder.
2. Click "Mail" in the menu bar in the upper left corner of the screen.
3. Click Favorites.

4. If you have not already done so, click the "General" tab.

5. Click the drop-down menu next to "Sound for new messages."

6. When you receive a new message, click the sound you want to hear. Every time you click a sound, it is played first.

Mail Settings: how to add a signature

An email signature is what appears under the body of each email you send: when you customize an email signature, you do not need to type your name again at the end of the email.

1. Launch Email from Dock or Finder.
2. tap "Mail" in the menu bar at the upper left of the screen.
3. Choose preferences.
4. Select the signature tab.

5. Click on the account you want to add a signature to.
6. Select the + button at the bottom of the window.
7. Enter your signature in the right pane. You can do whatever you want.
8. Click in the center window to change the signature name.
9. Select the drop-down menu next to Signature Selection.
   10. Click on an option:
   ◦ No.

- ◦ The signature you just created
- ◦ Random
- ◦ To

Mail Settings: how to send new emails

1. Launch Email from Dock or Finder.
2. Click the write button.
3. Enter the email address of the person to whom you want to send the message. You can enter multiple email addresses.
4. Enter an email subject.
5. Type the body of your email.
6. Click the send button. The top left of the message window looks like a paper plane.

Mail Settings: how to reply to emails

If you receive an email, you may need to reply. The answer is as follows:

1. Launch Email from Dock or Finder.
2. Click the email you want to reply to.
3. Click the "Answer" button, it looks like a curved arrow. If the email has multiple recipients, you can also choose to reply to all of them, but click the "reply all" button, which looks like two curved arrows. If you want to share an email with others, you can also send an email by clicking the forward button (right arrow next to the answer button).
4. Write and send an email.

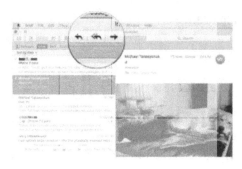

Mail settings: how to view and download email attachments

Part of the fun of sending and receiving emails is getting photos and videos, especially those too big to be sent via iMessage. Usually, pictures appear directly in the email, but you can also download them.

1. Launch Email from Dock or Finder.
2. Open the email containing the attachment you want to download.
3. Double-click the document in the body of the email to view it. The image usually appears on the body email setup: How to search for specific email messages
4. Click the search bar on the top right of the window.
5. Type your search query. It can be an email address, topic, name, or even just exact words from an email.
6. Optionally click a search option in the drop-down that appears.

Mail settings: how to search for specific emails

1. Launch the "Mail" app from the dock station or Finder
2. Click the search bar at the top right of the window.
3. Enter your search query. It could be an email address, title, name, or just a specific name in an email.

4. (Optional) Click the search option in the drop-down menu that appears.

5. (Optional) Click the folder to search. You can search for certain folders or just search them all.
6. Click the email you want to open.

Mail Settings: How to filter emails unread

If you receive a lot of emails, it can be difficult to keep track of what you have read and what you have not read. But this is not necessary. You can filter emails by "Unread".

1. Launch Mail from the Finder port.
2. Click View in the menu bar at the top left of the screen.
3. Select the filter method.
4. Select unread.

Alternatively, you can click the filter button next to "Filter by" at the top of the "Inbox" section. By default, it will only show unread emails.

Mail settings: how to mark emails as unread

If you want to revisit the email, but do not want to lose it, you can mark it as unread to show it at the top of your inbox.

1. Launch Email from Dock or Finder.
2. Right-click the email you want to mark as unread.
3. Click Mark as unread.

Or, if you have a magic mouse, you can swipe directly into the email and click "Unread" on your iPhone or iPad.

Mail settings: how to delete emails

After a while, your inbox can be very full. Get rid of the clutter you do not need!

1. Launch Email from Dock or Finder.
2. Click the email you want to delete. If you want to delete more messages, you can click one, hold the Shift key and then click another. All messages within each click message will be selected. If you do not want to delete messages further, you can hold the command while clicking. tap the delete switch at the top of the window. This is a trash can.

You can also right-click the inbox and click delete, or, if you have magic mice, you can swipe left and click the trash.

Music

The Apple Music app allows you to easily organize and enjoy purchased iTunes Store purchases, songs and albums in your database and the Apple Music catalog (allowing you to listen to millions of songs when you want them) Click to watch the following content, tracks played previous and playable content words. Buy the music you want in the iTunes Store.

It's on your bookshelf. You can easily view and play items purchased in the iTunes Store, items added to the Apple Music catalog, and music in your database. Sort your content by newly added artist, artist, album, or song.

Browse the best Apple Music. Click "Browse" in the sidebar to view new music and special versions of Apple Music, a monthly music streaming service. Stream and download over 50 million songs, no ads, and select from multiple playlists to get the best mix at any time.

Sing together. Click the "English" button on the toolbar to display a panel containing the lyrics of the current song (if any).

Listen. Click "Radio" in the sidebar to listen to Apple Music 1 live streaming or listen to any episode in the Apple Music series. Explore channels for almost all genres of music.

Ask Siri. Say the same thing: "Play Apple Music 1."

Easily sync. Sync your music content directly to the Apple Music app. When the device is connected, you will see it in the Finder sidebar. Just drag the content you need to the device. You can also back up and restore devices to Finder.

Shop in the iTunes Store. If you want to have music, click the iTunes Store on the sidebar. (If you do not see the store in the sidebar, select "Music"> "Favorites", click "General", then click on "Show iTunes Store.")

Tip: When the screen space is very valuable, please switch to MiniPlayer to open a small floating window, you can drag it to the desired location to listen and control the music while performing other tasks on your Mac. To open MiniPlayer, select Window> MiniPlayer.

Use the touch bar. When playing a song, you'll see a rewind, playback/pause, and quick forward buttons on the touch bar.

News
Apple News is a one-stop-shop, one of the most trusted news and editors selected and personalized. You can save the article for later reading, or read it offline or on other devices. Apple News + allows you to read hundreds of magazines, popular newspapers, and leading digital publishers for one month's price.

Note: Apple News and Apple News + are not available in all countries or regions.

Customize your feed. Follow your favorite channels and topics to view them in the "Today" feed and sidebar. Enter the media or articles in the search field and click the "Apply" button to track.

Tip: If you are reading an article and want to save it for later use, select "File"> "Save Story". To view the article later, click "Saved News" near the top of the sidebar. If you sign in with the same Apple ID, you can access the article on any device.

Garage Band

GarageBand app is for creating, recording, and sharing music. It has your recording studio at home and everything you need to learn to play a musical instrument, write music, or record songs.

Create a new project. You can start from the song template, select the speed, keys, and other options, then click "Record" and start playing. Create your song — for example, use different tracks and loops Click Quick Help and hover the mouse pointer over objects to understand what they are and how they work.

Rhythm. You can use Drummer Loops to quickly add drums to your project. Click "Loop Browser", then drag "Drummer Loop" to the empty "Track" area. You can customize the drum loop to fit your song with a simple set of controls.

Record your voice. Select "Songs"> "New Track", then select the microphone under "Audio". Click the triangle next to "Details" to set input, output, and monitoring options, then click "Create". Click the "Record" button to start recording, or click the "Play" button to stop recording.

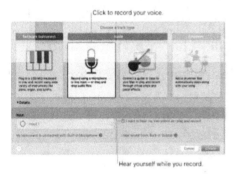

Use the touch bar. Easily adjust the smart controls of the selected track. Tap the button to fine-tune the ringtone, turn on or off effects, or adjust the volume of the audio track.

Tips and tricks

Install iPhone and iPad apps

The M1 SoC uses the same construction and A-series chips on the iPhone and iPad. This means you can finally run iPhone and iPad apps locally on the M1 MacBook Air and Pro.

Go to the Mac App Mass, search for an app (such as Overcast or Facebook), and switch to the "iPhone and iPad apps" tab. You can then select the iPhone / iPad app, install it like any other app on your Mac, and open it with a Spotlight search or with a touchpad.

Catch; The developer should make the iPhone and iPad app versions available on Mac, so you may not see popular apps (like Instagram or Gmail) in the Mac App Store.

You can also show a list of purchased/installed apps on iPhone and iPad. Just select your profile from the bottom left corner of the Mac App Store and switch to the "iPhone and iPad Apps" tab to access it. After that, start installing the required applications.

Look for other ways to touch

All the iPhone and iPad apps you can install on your Mac are designed for use on the touch screen your M1 MacBook does not have this feature. As a solution, Apple used something called a "touch substitute". It is a combination of trackpad touch and keyboard buttons that can be used to communicate with these apps. You can call the preset commands by selecting the "Touch Overlay" option in the menu bar of the app-based touch.

Adjust the background light of the keyboard

If you want to adjust the keyboard brightness of the M1 MacBook Air, you will no longer see related access controls. Instead, you should use the control center for this (this is one of the great new additions to macOS Big Sur).

Just click the "Control Center" icon at the top right of the menu bar. After that, select the keyboard light and move the left or right lighting slide to increase or decrease the brightness.

Insert icons in the menu bar

As you may have noticed, the Control Center separates almost all the previously existing icons from the menu bar. This keeps things in order, but because you have to go deeper into the control center, accessing the Wi-Fi or Bluetooth menus is also difficult.

Thankfully, you don't have to endure it, just drag the icon out of the Control Center, and return it to the menu bar. This also applies to controls such as "Brightness of the keyboard" and "Display".

Appointment, recognition, and non-interference

Apple may have discarded the keyboard background from the M1 MacBook Air feature line, but the same keys point to other useful features of macOS. You can now use "Dictation" and "Do Not Disturb" by pressing F5 and F6 respectively. Besides, the F4 key (which had previously launched launchpad) can now deliver Spotlight search.

Put it to sleep

The M1 chip is a beast. Close and open the lid, and your MacBook Air or Pro should wake up quickly, like the iPhone and iPad. This gives you enough reason to put it to sleep to save battery life.

In other words, the service life of M1 MacBooks is a few hours longer than that of Intel models (18 and 20 hours of video playing time for Air and Pro models respectively), so even if you can take a breather all-day Keep running all day.

Show the battery percentage

Speaking of battery life, by default, the M1 MacBook Air and Pro will not display the battery percentage in the menu bar. This is a design decision made by Apple on macOS Big Sur, and it usually works on all MacBooks. If you want to check the battery percentage, you should now bring up the "Battery Status" menu by selecting the battery indicator.

However, you can return the battery percentage indicator to the menu bar if needed. To do this, open the Apple menu, select "System Favorites", and click the "Dock & Menu Bar" icon. After that, switch to the "Battery" sidebar and check the box next to "Show percentage."

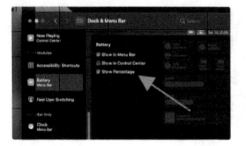

Check battery usage statistics

macOS Big Sur also introduced a new battery panel, which shows battery usage statistics, such as the iPhone and iPad. You can do this by selecting the "Battery" icon in the "System Favorites" window. This can be useful if the battery in your M1 MacBook starts to discharge immediately and you don't know why. The "Battery" panel also contains "Energy Saver" settings from the first macOS duplication.

Set highlight color

If you're tired of seeing the same blue buttons and symbols on the M1 MacBook Air or Pro, try making the content clearer by changing the Accent color. Scroll to the "System Favorites" window, select "General", and select your favorite color from the "Emphasis" tab. You should immediately notice changes in all areas.

Change accent marks to multicolor

The macOS Big Sur also comes with a "multi-colored" option located to the left of the "Accent" button under "System Favorites"> "General". Select it, each program can have its color scheme.

Disable wallpaper color

If you do not like the background tones on your old MacBook, you can no longer tolerate it. Go to System Preferences> General>, and uncheck the option to allow Windows to set the wallpaper tone.

Manage notifications immediately

macOS Big Sur comes with an advanced notification center. Notifications are now packed with the app, making it easier to manage. Best of all, and you can manage notifications directly.

Right-click on a notification stack or specific application. Then, select "Send in peace" to send notifications silently to the "Notification Center", or click "Close" to disable future alerts for this application.

Check the M1 compatibility of the application

Not all apps you install on the M1 MacBook Air or Pro are designed for Apple Silicon. However, the M1 chip is so fast that it can easily run Intel-coded programs with the Rosetta 2 Translation Environment integrated. However, applications for these two chips (Apple likes to call them "Universal") should quickly launch on the M1 MacBook Air and work much better.

To check if a particular application has traditional M1 chip support, start by going to the "Applications" folder in Finder. After that, right-click on the app and select the "Get Info" context menu option. If you see "Application (General)" next to "Category", the application is configured for chip M1. If you look for "Application (Intel)" instead, the application will work in a version rendered by Rosetta 2.

Keep your app up to date

If you have non-global applications on your Mac, please be sure to update them regularly, as they may provide native Apple Silicon support as soon as possible. Go to the Mac App Store and switch to the "Updates" tab to install the latest updates. If you downloaded an app outside the Mac App Store, try finding the update option within the app.

Manage and edit widgets

macOS Big Sur comes with iPhone-like widgets, and you can access them via the notification center on your M1 MacBook Air or Pro. Although you can't drag them to the desktop or place them on top of each other, you can add a widget library to add and remove widgets, and easily choose between different sizes. To do this, use the "Edit Widget" option at the bottom of the notifications center.

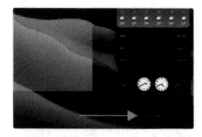

Additionally, you can right-click on any widget and switch between sizes without dragging it down to the widget library. For some widgets, you have a right-click menu option for "Edit widget", which lets you change the function of the widget. For example, you can use it to change the time zone in the "World Clock" widget.

Install third-party widgets

You can also download third-party applications with the help of the widget by simply jumping into the App Store. If you hate hunting around the App Store, check out this Apple-selected theme.

Start using Safari again

On macOS Big Sur, Safari has achieved significant performance improvements, making it 50% faster than Chrome. The situation is much better on the M1 MacBook, where you can open multiple tabs without stopping. If you are using a performance test like Chrome, please consider giving Safari another chance.

Watch YouTube in 4K

Safari also supports YouTube in 4K. As we all know, the M1 chip on the MacBook is so fast that it can handle most 2160p video streaming without effort.

Customize Safari

Finally, Safari comes with a customized "start" page that allows you to easily add your personality. Just select the "Custom" icon in the lower right corner of the screen, and you can quickly enable or disable "Favorites", "frequent access", "privacy reports" and other components. Additionally, you can also add a background to the "Start Page" - select one from a set of built-in domains or upload your image.

Edit videos in the photo app

Good video streaming in M1 MacBook Air or Pro is best for iMovie or Final Cut Pro. However, if you are fast, the "Photos" app on macOS Big Sur should be able to help you. You now have access to the entire set of editing options that were previously reserved for photos only. Switch to "Edit" mode while watching the video to try it out.

Bring up-to-date your M1 MacBook Air or Pro

The M1 MacBook Air and M1 MacBook Pro are amazing devices. However, they are relatively new, so you will encounter all of these problems if you continue to use them, there will be many errors, inefficiencies, and stability issues. Therefore, please be sure to get the latest software updates as soon as they become available (usually resolving known issues).

macOS Big Sur also makes additional updates faster and more impactful, so you no longer have reason to undo them. To update your Mac, go to "System Preferences"> "Software Updates" and apply all updates (if any). If you want your Mac to update itself, you can check the box next to "Automatically update my Mac".

www.ingramcontent.com/pod-product-compliance
Lightning Source LLC
LaVergne TN
LVHW051335050326
832903LV00031B/3551